THE ANGLO-BOER WAR
1899–1902

THE
ANGLO-BOER WAR

1899–1902

G.D. Scholtz

Protea Book House
Pretoria
2000

The Anglo-Boer War 1899–1902
G.D. Scholtz

First English edition, first impression 2000
ISBN 1-919825-12-6
Originally published in 1960 as
Die Tweede Vryheidsoorlog 1899–1902
Second Afrikaans edition, Protea Boekhuis, 1998

Protea Book House
PO Box 35110
Menlo Park 0102
protea@intekom.co.za

Design and typography by HOND BK
Layout by ANTWORKS Layout & Design
Maps by Magda Geringer
Translation into English by Bridget Theron
Cover, title page and margin illustrations by Anton Hoffman from:
Die Transvaaler im Krieg mit England — Kriegserinnerungen
von General Ben Viljoen
J.F. Lehmanns Verlag, München, 1902
Photographs with permission of the
War Museum of the Boer Republics, Bloemfontein
The illustration on p. 55 (The battle of Paardeberg)
was provided by courtesy of Prof. C.J. Barnard

Reproduction by Dusk Dimensions
Printed and bound by ABC Press, Durban

Preface to the English edition

In 1957 a competition to write a suitable school textbook on the Anglo-Boer War was launched by the board of the South African Academy for Science and Art. The prize was awarded to Dr Gert Daniel Scholtz, historian and former chief editor of the Afrikaans daily newspaper, *Die Transvaler* (1958–1968).

Gert Scholtz was born in Philipstown on 15 August 1905. He published a wide range of historical works including the monumental, eight-volume *Die Ontwikkeling van die Politieke Denke van die Afrikaner* which was originally planned to run to ten volumes. He died on 13 July 1983 from complications connected with Parkinson's disease.

His celebrated manuscript *Die Tweede Vryheidsoorlog*, somewhat expanded and with minor alterations, appeared in 1960 and was published by Voortrekkerpers. In the first edition Scholtz said that the work did not claim to be a comprehensive study, and that it only discussed the most important events and information on the war.

After a number of years during which the book was unavailable, the publisher decided to modernise the language and to bring out another Afrikaans edition in 1998. No changes were made to the factual information which appeared in Scholtz's original manuscript.

With interest in the Anglo-Boer War running high in these centenary years, an English translation seemed the next logical step. Again, there has been no tampering with the factual material and the only major change has been in the title. The name of the war which took place in South Africa in 1899–1902 has become the subject of rigorous debate and most historians now agree that the most appropriate and historically accurate name is the Anglo-Boer War. This is not to deny the part played by black South Africans in the encounter — this has been established beyond doubt — but the two main combatants were certainly the British and the republicans.

Scholtz, inspired by a fierce Afrikaner nationalism which was riding the crest of the wave in South Africa in the prosperity of the 1950s and 1960s, predictably saw the war in a very particular light. In his view the Boers in the two republics were fighting not only to maintain their political independence but also their values, their attitudes and their way of life. Unlike later historians, he saw no sinister materialist motives, no interplay of capitalism in the struggle: he saw it as motivated purely by political aspirations. For Scholtz it was the mighty, greedily expansionist Britain against the innocent, valiant little Boer republics who wanted nothing more than to be left alone to enjoy their hard won independence.

It was these sentiments that inspired this interesting book on a fascinating war. More than forty years down the line the work is still a good read with its many strong points, some weaknesses and several obvious omissions. And while the spirit of Scholtz's writing has been retained in the subject matter translated here, some of the terminology and capitalisation (republican instead of Republican, for example), and the outworn title, have been updated.

CONTENTS

CHAPTER I
THE PRELUDE TO THE WAR

The outbreak of war

In South Africa in the last years of the nineteenth century there was a direct confrontation between two political aspirations: British imperialism and Afrikaner nationalism.

The proponents of the first ideal wanted to unite the entire South Africa under the British flag, and the presence of two independent Boer republics, the Transvaal (South African Republic or SAR) and the Orange Free State, was an obstacle to the attainment of this goal. They were anxious to put these republics under British control. Afrikaner nationalists, on the other hand, aimed to strengthen and even expand their republics and for this reason they were certainly not prepared to become part of a united South Africa under British rule.

A new phase in the struggle between these two ideals was reached in 1886 with the discovery of gold on the Witwatersrand in the Transvaal. Thousands of immigrants, most of them British subjects, flocked to the goldfields to try their luck. Justifiably, the Transvalers saw the arrival of so many people as a threat to their independence and in 1890 they made the requirements to become eligible for citizenship so much stricter that outsiders could only qualify after fourteen years of residence. The majority of British subjects had no plans to give up their citizenship but nevertheless began to demand some voice in the government of the Transvaal Republic on the grounds that they contributed the bulk of its income. To give expression to their demands, the Uitlanders (as they came to be known) even formed their own political movement, the *Transvaal National Union.*

The tension reached a dramatic climax at the end of 1895. Cecil John Rhodes, Prime Minister of the Cape Colony and founder of the *Chartered*

Cecil John Rhodes

Company which managed Rhodesia (now Zimbabwe and Zambia) contacted a few leading Uitlanders and gradually a conspiracy was hatched to instigate an uprising in Johannesburg, upon the start of which Dr L.S. Jameson, a friend of Rhodes, would then rush in with a force of a few hundred soldiers to provide assistance.

The raid took place in the closing days of 1895. Before Jameson could reach Johannesburg, the most important town on the Witwatersrand, he was intercepted by the Boer commandos and forced to surrender.

The unsuccessful raid naturally caused a huge political storm which led *inter alia* to Rhodes's resignation as prime minister of the Cape Colony. President S.J.P. Kruger of the Transvaal, who acted with considerable magnanimity in his victory hour, made certain concessions to the Uitlanders – including the establishment of a municipal board for Johannesburg. However, this did nothing to diminish the estrangement between the Afrikaners and the Uitlanders.

The dissatisfaction of the Uitlanders also had repercussions in Britain. The Minister of Colonies, Joseph Chamberlain, took particular note of this. As a statesman who was involved on a daily basis with world issues, he was convinced that powers such as America, Germany, France and Russia were poised to challenge Britain's supremacy.

Chamberlain was of the opinion that the British position could only be maintained by making the colonies politically and economically dependent upon the motherland. This was why he began to pay so much attention to South Africa. Only when the whole of South Africa was under British control would the situation be entirely secure.

In order to realise his goals more effectively, Chamberlain decided to appoint Sir Alfred Milner, who held similar opinions on these matters, as governor of the Cape Colony and British high commissioner in South Africa.

Milner arrived in South Africa in May 1897. As early as March 1898 he referred to the clash between the Uitlanders and the Transvaal government in a speech in Graaff-Reinet, blaming the Transvaal for refusing to grant political rights to the Uitlanders.

The situation was now becoming progressively more tense. In December 1898 a British subject, a man called Edgar, was shot dead in Johannesburg by a police constable in the course of his duties. Although it was clear that the constable had acted in self-defence, the *South African League*, a new political organisation, seized upon the opportunity to submit a petition outlining the Uitlander grievances and signed by several thousand Uitlanders to the British queen. In this way a link was forged between the Uitlanders and the British government.

In a letter to the British government Milner insisted that there must be some intervention because the Transvaal was undermining the British position in South Africa. President M.T. Steyn of the Orange Free State, already fearful that war was about to break out, made an attempt to rescue the situation. He invited Kruger and Milner to meet in Bloemfontein to discuss the whole Uitlander issue around the conference table. Accordingly, these two met in the Free State capital on 31 May 1899.

Joseph Chamberlain

Kruger was prepared to grant the franchise to the Uitlanders after residence of seven years. Milner held out for five years, and when Kruger refused, Milner broke off all negotiations.

After his return to Cape Town, Milner immediately requested the British government to strengthen the garrison in South Africa, and thousands of soldiers were promptly sent to South Africa. In the months that followed, they took up positions at Mafeking and Kimberley in the Cape Colony and at Dundee and Ladysmith in Natal. They were thus deployed close to the borders of the two republics.

While the British troops were arriving, further negotiations were taking place between the British and the Transvaal governments on the question of the Uitlander franchise. But Chamberlain's demands were of such a nature that their acceptance would place the independence of the Transvaal in jeopardy. The tension continued to rise. By the end of September the burgher commandos were called up and sent to the front. On either side of the borders there were now armed troops.

13

President Paul Kruger

Once President Steyn had been consulted, the Transvaal government issued an ultimatum to the British government, demanding that they withdraw their troops within 48 hours. If this demand was not met, a state of war would ensue between Britain and the two republics. The British government refused to accede and on 11 October 1899 the war in South Africa began.

The two opposing parties

Before embarking on a description of the war, it is necessary to look briefly at how the two Boer republics and Britain were organised for the encounter.

As is still the case in countries that are at war, both sides conducted the struggle according to their previous experience in combat.

• *The two republics* – Since the days of the Great Trek the Afrikaners of the two republics had been involved almost continuously in conflict with one or more groups of black people. These wars helped them to develop a particular pattern of military strategy. The basis of this was the commando system which originated as early as the eighteenth century. The Boer would set out for combat with his rifle and his horse and would place himself, along with his friends and acquaintances from the district, under the control of a commandant. Accustomed to a free-living existence, the Boer knew no discipline – something that would cost him dearly when he was pitted against disciplined troops. However, to a significant extent the Boer made up for this lack of discipline in the field. There was nobody who knew how to use the terrain better than he. During a clash the Boer was more often than not out of sight to his opponents. Virtually every Boer was an excellent shot and with deadly accuracy he could maintain his fire, inflicting heavy losses on the enemy.

After his rifle, the Boer on commando depended upon his horse, and as a rider he was unsurpassed. This gave him a mobility that, prior to the era of mechanised vehicles, was simply bewildering. A mounted burgher could always cover a much greater distance than the British foot soldier.

14

The wars against the African people, who could easily lure a mounted commando into an ambush and cut it off, had taught the Boer to use his ox wagon as a means of defence. When the burghers were surrounded by black warriors the ox wagons were placed in a circle and by using them as cover, the enemy assaults could be repulsed. Although the use of wagons naturally impeded the mobility of the commandos considerably, the Boers became so accustomed to going into battle with their wagons that it was a tactic they would also employ against the British. At the outset, when speed and mobilty might have helped the commandos to penetrate deep into enemy territory, the wagons were indeed a serious hindrance.

The Boer was not a professional soldier and, in addition, was usually the head of a family that was dependant upon him. He was thus loathe to expose himself to unnecessary danger on the front. Then too, because his previous opponents had been Africans whose resources such as food supplies were usually limited, the Afrikaners often preferred to follow a strategy of wearing down the enemy, whereas a determined charge might well on occasion have inflicted heavy losses and given the burghers a quick victory.

President Marthinus Theunis Steyn

The Afrikaners preferred instead to besiege the black people and force them to surrender because of starvation. These tactics were also used against the British, with disastrous results for the republican forces.

The Boers' lack of military training was also apparent among the officers. The fact that they were elected by popular vote was a serious flaw, because this often meant that men who were ill-equipped for the task were appointed.

The commandants and field cornets, who only served in their military capacity in time of war, obviously knew little about military matters and were thus at a distinct disadvantage when pitted against one of the foremost world powers. Each war brings outstanding leaders to the fore: men who know what decisions need to be taken, and so it was with the Afrikaners. The war against Britain produced its De Wet, Botha, De la Rey, Kemp, Beyers, Muller and others. It was these men who earned the Afrikaner his great renown as a combatant.

The Afrikaner, despite his background, was indeed able to adapt to military discipline. Proof of this was the Artillery Corps of the two republics and the Transvaal Police Corps. In terms of discipline, even in the most intense combat, these soldiers acquitted themselves just as creditably as members of any other army.

• *Britain* – In most cases the Britons who came to South Africa to take part in the war were professional soldiers. All the officers had chosen the life of the soldier as their career, while the ordinary soldiers were by and large those who had served in the army for a number of years and were accustomed to strict military discipline. This was the most significant difference between the British soldier and the ordinary burgher on the republican side.

The British soldier's discipline was his strength, but in a certain sense also his weakness. Orders issued to him during the most hectic battles were obeyed blindly – even if this meant laying down his life – and this probably led to many victories. But the strict discipline also destroyed the British soldier's individuality. While the burgher knew instinctively what to do in a skirmish, the soldier was dependent in every respect on his officers. He was able to do only what he was ordered to do and as sharpshooter he was also nowhere near as good as a burgher.

Previously, the British army had been made up mainly of soldiers on foot, or infantry men. There were also horsemen, that is cavalry, but their numbers were limited. The preponderance of foot soldiers meant that the British army did not at first have the mobility of the commandos. A commando could move almost three or four times faster than a British column and this was a distinct advantage for the commandos. Only later in the war did the British army command alter their tactics and make greater use of mounted divisions.

The British army was at all times far better equipped with artillery than were the commandos. This immediately tipped the scales in Britain's favour.

The British soldier came to fight in a country that was completely unknown to him. He knew practically nothing of the climate, the geography, or the vegetation of South Africa, so at first he did not know how to find the necessary cover on the battlefield. Because of this, he was inclined to expose himself to the burghers' fire and often his opponents were completely hidden.

At first, the British army command also found it difficult to adapt to

South African conditions. From the time of the Crimean War, which ended in 1856, until the end of the nineteenth century – with the exception of the First War of Independence in 1880–81– Britain had been involved only in a number of colonial wars against African people. Suddenly the British army came up against a war which demanded the ultimate use of all its capabilities and the British officers were unequal to the task. This became very obvious in their many failures at the beginning of the war. If the republican military leaders made serious errors, this was no less true of the professional British officers. Only when they had an overwhelming number of troops at their disposal were they able to reach their goal.

•*The difference* – The most important difference between the two opposing parties was indeed their numerical strength. At the beginning of the war the two republics could only, at most, muster only 60 000 men. This number was probably marginally increased by the addition of Cape and Natal Afrikaners who subsequently joined the commandos. But every burgher who died in the field or who was taken prisoner meant a weakening of the republican forces.

The opposite was true of the British troops. The British army command originally thought that a relatively small force would be sufficient to defeat the two republics. It soon became evident that this was a grave miscalculation, whereupon the size of the army was quickly increased to about 250 000 men. This made it approximately four times bigger than the highest estimate of the number of burghers. It was this overwhelming numerical superiority which decided the war in favour of Britain.

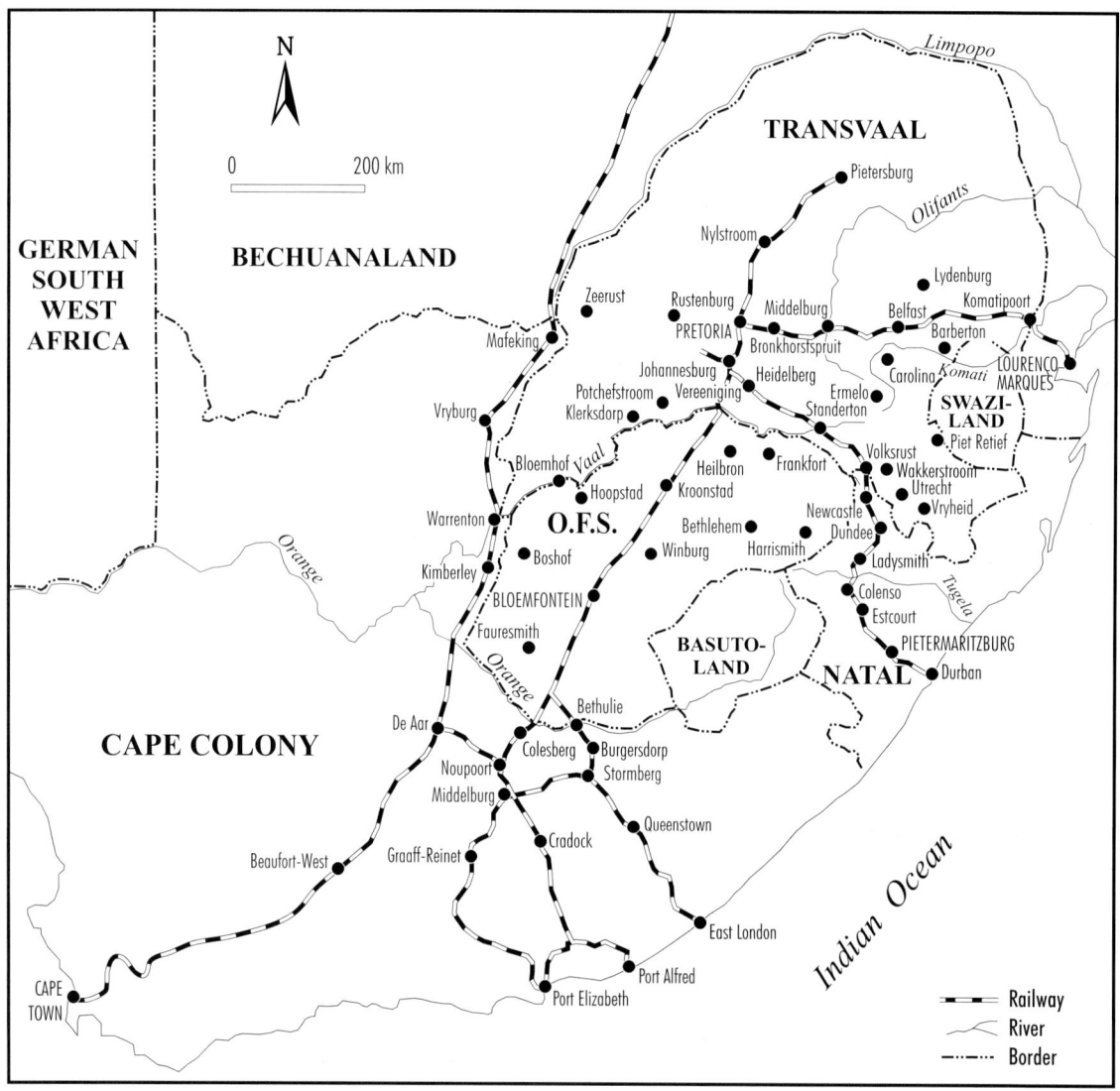

Map of the theatre of War, October 1899

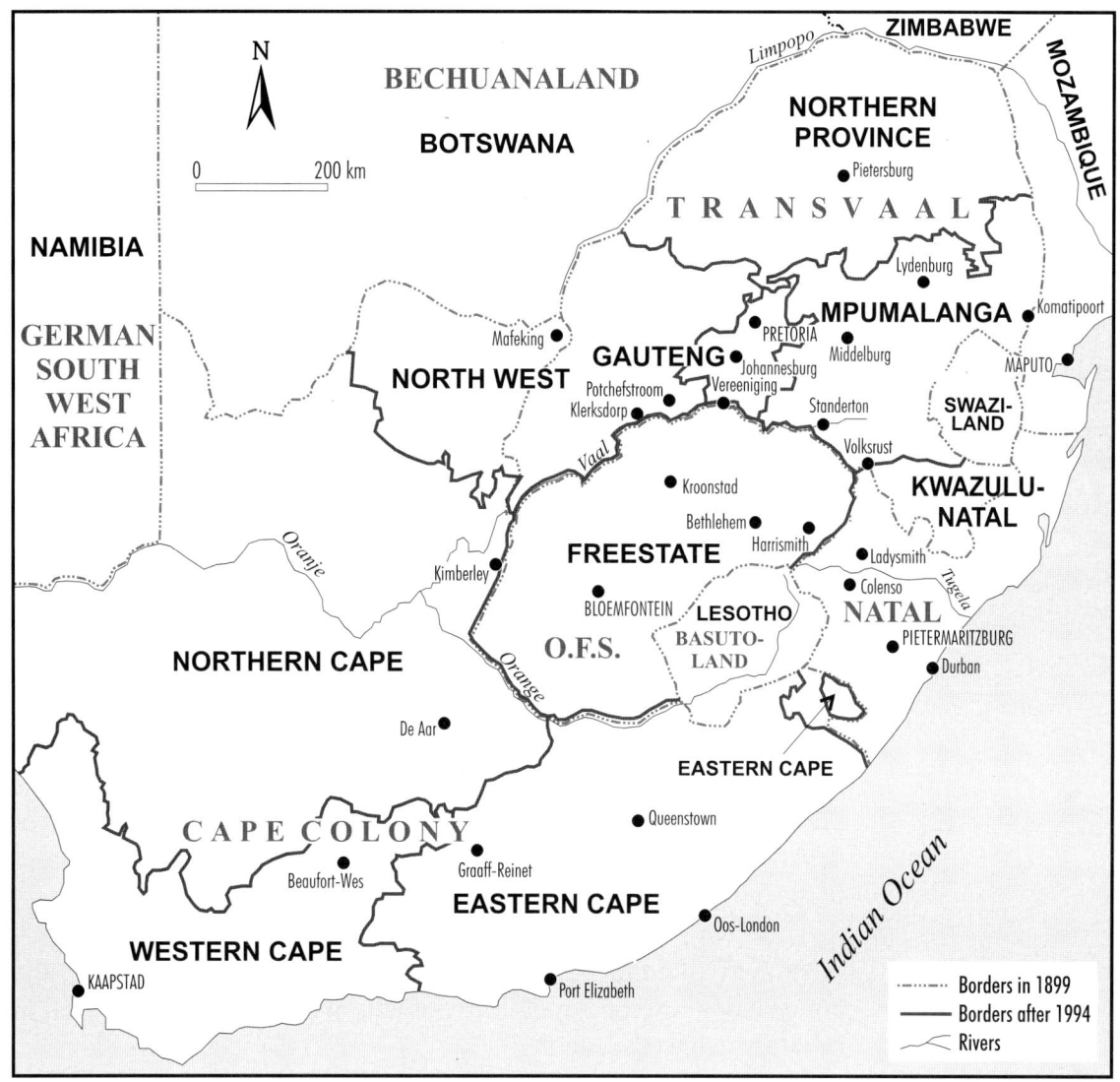

Modern South Afrika

General Penn Symons

CHAPTER II

THE REPUBLICAN OFFENSIVE

When the war began on 11 October 1899 a large part of the British army was still at sea. Other divisions had not even left for South Africa. The British army command decided that the troops which were already deployed near the republics should adopt a defensive stance and wait until the reinforcements arrived.

When this superior force became available, they could immediately go onto the attack and the war could be brought to a successful conclusion by defeating the two republics within a few months.

The fact that the British were not able to assemble a large force at the outset, gave the republican forces an opportunity which they should have used to the full if they had hopes of winning the war. They should have gone on the offensive immediately after the declaration of war, destroyed the British forces deployed near the borders and then quickly advanced to the most important harbour towns in order to prevent more British troops from landing.

A strategy like this demanded that plans be made quickly, that the commandos be kept as mobile as possible and that very decisive action be taken against the enemy.

THE NATAL FRONT

The evolvement of the offensive

When the war broke out the British forces in Natal were stationed at Dundee and Ladysmith. At Dundee there were slightly fewer than 4 000 men under General Penn Symons. General White was in command of the more than 8 000 men at Ladysmith.

The numerical strength of the Transvaal commandos which were to take part in the attack was apparently no more than 11 000. They

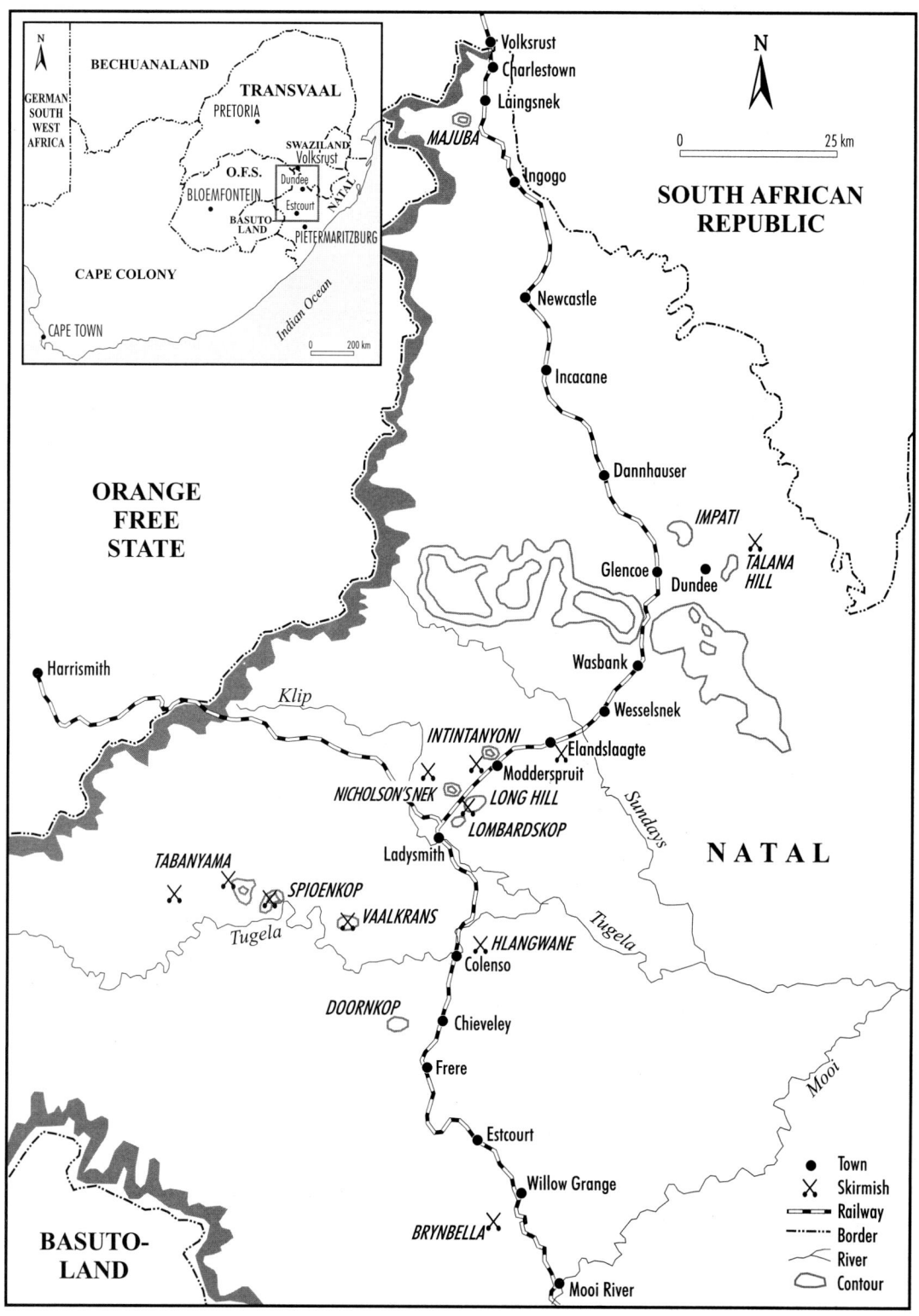

The Natal front 1899–1900

21

Commandant-General Piet Joubert

would be led by Commandant-General P.J. Joubert himself. There were also several Free State commandos, numbering about 4 000 men, who were drawn up to the west of the Drakensberg Mountains.

Joubert's first task was to attack and destroy the British force at Dundee and then to combine the Transvaal and Free State commandos. When he had done this he could turn his attention to defeating the force at Ladysmith which would open the way for the republicans to go through to Pietermaritzburg and Durban.

In order to reach this objective, it was crucial to act very quickly before the British reinforcements arrived. But Joubert was not a man to take snap decisions; he was by nature far too cautious. At the beginning of the war he was already 67 years of age and he was unequal to the task of accepting this heavy responsibility. Instead of immediately moving mobile mounted commandos deep into Natal, cutting off the British communications and attacking them in an aggressive manner, Joubert hesitated from the outset, delaying unnecessarily at a time when every hour counted.

The result was that more than a week passed before the republican forces even came to blows with their opponents.

Dundee

Joubert devised a clever plan for the attack on the British forces at Dundee and if it had been executed properly, it would have led to a convincing victory. He divided his forces into three divisions. The first division, which was under General L.J. Meyer, had to attack Dundee from the east. This division had to take possession of Talana Hill and Lennox Hill. The second division would be under General D.J.E. Erasmus and had to attack Dundee from a northerly direction. This implied that Impati Mountain had to be occupied. The third division under the command of J.H.M. Kock had to move southwards and cut off the rail link between Dundee and Ladysmith so that no help could be brought in. The plan naturally demanded close co-operation between the troops under Meyer and Erasmus. Further, it was crucial that Kock, who had only a small force, should avoid all contact with the British garrison at Ladysmith.

Because of the inefficiency of his sub-ordinates, very little of Joubert's strategy went according to plan. Early in the morning of 20 October, Meyer's commandos were at the appointed place and likewise Erasmus and his men had occupied Impati Mountain. However, there was mist over the summit of the mountain and Erasmus decided that this was reason enough to call off the attack. He waited there as quiet as a mouse and allowed Meyer to bear the full brunt of the enemy action.

The battle of Dundee began when the Transvaal artillery fired several shots into the British camp. This was more than enough to rouse the British soldiers' fighting spirit.

Under command of Penn Symons himself, they immediately went on the attack to drive their opponents from the two hills. It was at this point that Erasmus should have joined the fray, but he simply failed to do so. The result was that after a few hours Meyer's commandos were forced to flee and they retreated into Transvaal territory.

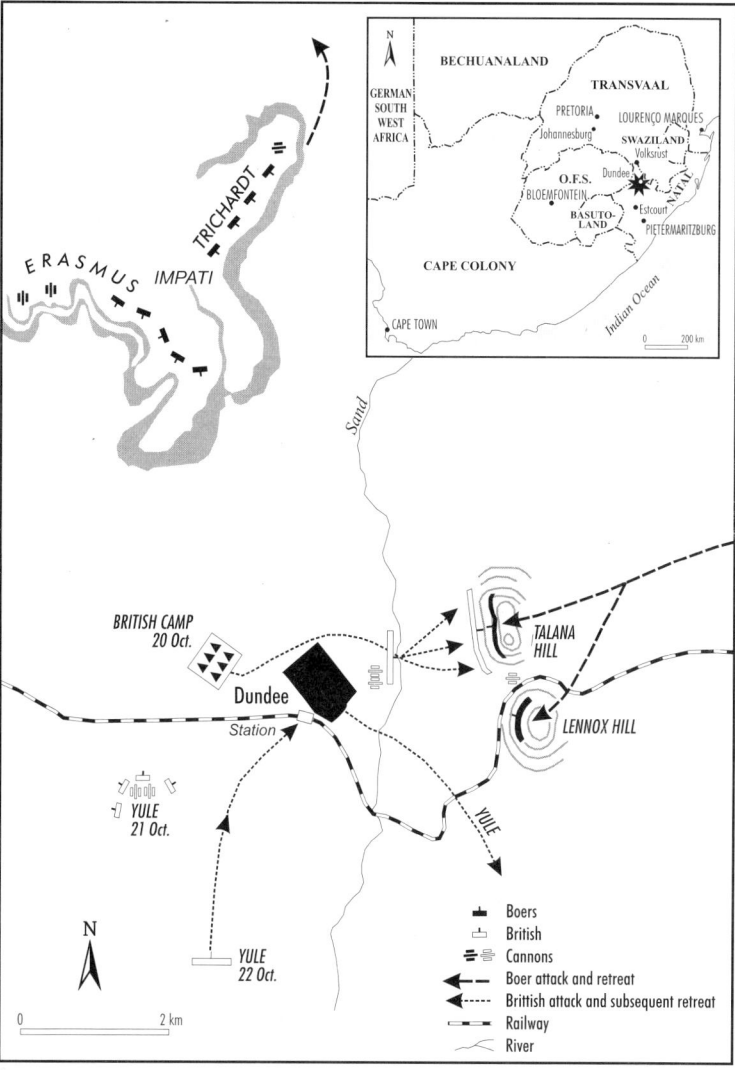

Dundee, 20 October 1899

The first skirmish in Natal thus ended in defeat for the Transvaal because of the poor showing of the commandants. But the British too had suffered very heavy losses and Penn Symons was mortally wounded. With so many commandos still in his immediate vicinity, General Yule, the new commander, found himself in a very difficult position and on the night of 22 to 23 October he thought it prudent to leave Dundee quietly and retreat to Ladysmith. It was only the next day that Joubert discovered that the enemy was no longer there.

The fiasco at Dundee cost the Boers dearly. The delay in destroying the British force meant that the desired result of this invasion of Natal, namely to break through to the coast, was unattainable. With the reinforcements that he received from Dundee, White, who was in Ladysmith, was now able to block the way through to the south and to hold back the invading commandos until new British troops could land in Durban.

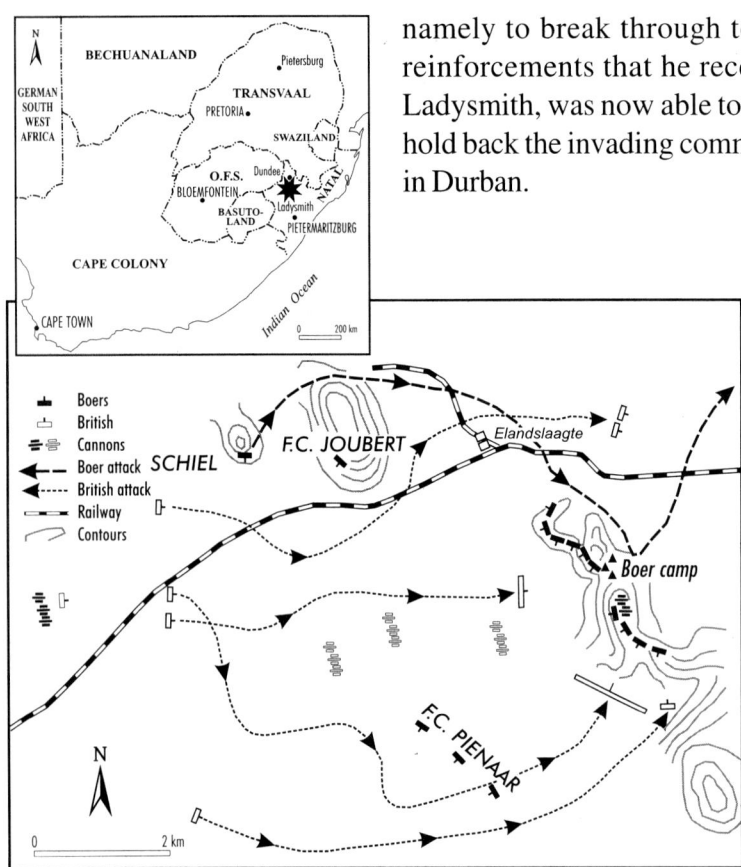

Elandslaagte, 21 October 1899

Elandslaagte

The day after the defeat at Dundee a second disaster hit the republican forces in Natal. Kock's commandos had carried out their orders to destroy the rail link between Dundee and Ladysmith.

But Kock was not satisfied with this and he proceeded to move further south. He even took the risk of occupying the railway station about 24 kilometres from Ladysmith. This was a very dangerous move because it placed him and his small number of men, which also included the German and Hollander Volunteer Corps, far too close to a large, hostile enemy force.

When White in Ladysmith heard of the arrival at Elandslaagte of such a weak republican force, he immediately decided to teach his opponent a severe lesson. On 21 October he dispatched a strong division of troops under General French to attack the enemy.

It would have been far better if Kock's men had retreated immediately they saw the British coming, but instead Kock chose to make a stand and start fighting. The outcome was exactly what was to be expected in such circumstances.

The British force achieved an overwhelming victory. The lancers in particular were able to mow down their fleeing opponents and Kock's force was practically annihilated. He himself was wounded, fell into the hands of the British and died a few days later in Ladysmith.

Rietfontein

The outcome of the battles at Dundee and Elandslaagte was a great setback for the republican forces. With the Transvalers bearing the brunt of the war, the Free State commandos meanwhile began to move carefully down along the Drakensberg Mountains, hoping to be able to make contact with Joubert's troops. The closer the Free Staters moved to Ladysmith, the more dangerous White's position became. He had to try to prevent the Free Staters and Transvalers from making contact. The best way to do this was to take on the Free Staters and try to drive them back. With this in mind he sent out a strong force, hoping to subject the Free Staters to the same fate as the Transvalers at Elandslaagte.

The Free Staters had anticipated the enemy attack and had taken up a position at Rietfontein north of Ladysmith. They were attacked there by the British on 24 October. But the Free State forces withstood their baptism of fire so well that the enemy, having tried in vain to drive them back, was forced to halt the attack after a few hours and return to Ladysmith without having achieved its goal.

Modderspruit and Nicholson's Nek

The evacuation of Dundee by the British and the victory at Rietfontein now meant that the republican forces could be combined. White gave no indication at all that he was going to leave Ladysmith and so a major confrontation between the two parties was unavoidable.

Joubert made a good choice of terrain for the expected clash. The combining of the Transvaal and Free State commandos meant that the republican troops could be drawn up in a crescent around Ladysmith from the south-east to the north. Ladysmith is surrounded by a number of hills and some of these, namely Umbulwana, Pepworth Hill and Nicholson's Nek were occupied by the Boers. White was in an invidious position because his opponents could so easily cut off his links to the south, to Pietermaritzburg and Durban. It was this possibility which influenced his decision to launch a major attack to drive the republican forces from their positions and to split the Transvalers and Free Staters again. His right wing would attack the Transvalers and force them back in an easterly direction. Then the main army would join the pursuit.

The left wing was given the task of cutting off the Transvalers from the Free Staters by occupying Nicholson's Nek.

At daybreak on 30 October the battle began with fierce artillery fire. The Transvaal cannons on Pepworth Hill suffered a particularly heavy assault, but the gunners showed that they possessed the necessary discipline and fought back as hard as they could. The fact that the British bombardment could make very little headway weakened their position considerably.

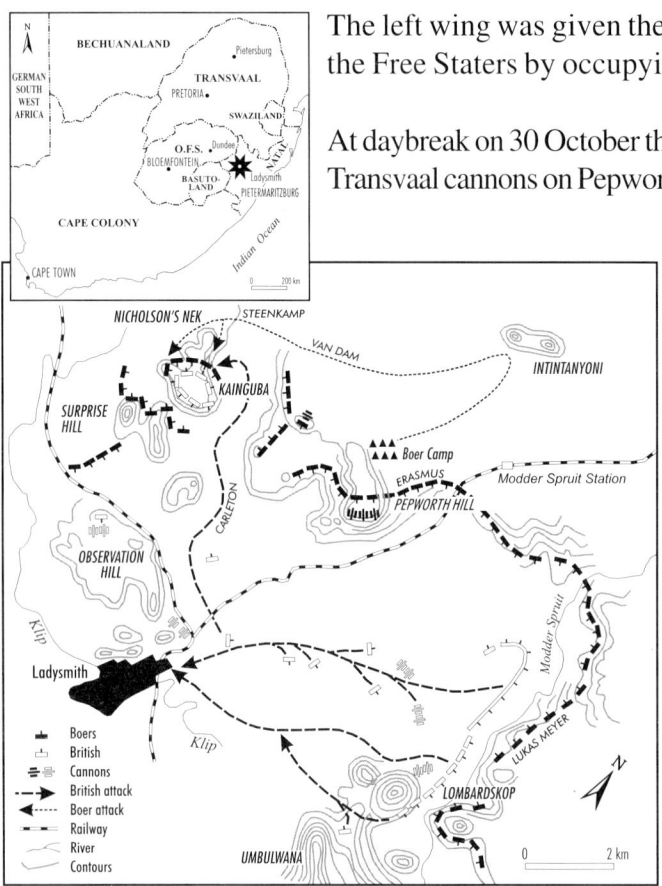

Battle of Nicholson's Nek and Modderspruit, 30 October 1899

Meanwhile the British right wing under Colonel Grimwood went on the attack. From the outset things went awry for him because the Transvalers were determined that they would not retreat. Before long they even began to get the better of the enemy and drove the British towards Ladysmith. By midday it was very clear that the attack by the British right wing had failed completely and the fighting was called off. On the Boer side an officer who was as yet unknown distinguished himself in this battle. He was later to become the famous General Louis Botha. This victory over the British right wing and main army came to be known as the battle of Modderspruit.

The British left wing under Colonel Carleton fared even worse. To begin with it looked as if the British were going to succeed in cutting off the Transvalers from the Free Staters because Nicholson's Nek had been occupied by British soldiers during the night without a blow being struck. This occurred because of the negligence of a commandant who was responsible for guarding this important post.

The sun was barely up when the presence of the British was discovered. An assistant field cornet from Heilbron immediately came forward to save the situation. He was the later General Christiaan de Wet. Under his inspired leadership a number of burghers scaled the ridge and managed to launch an attack. The British could not withstand these sharpshooters and a few hours later the white flag was raised. Several hundred soldiers were taken prisoner. Along the entire front – from Nicholson's Nek to Umbulwana – White had thus suffered a heavy defeat. His beaten, demoralised soldiers trailed back to Ladysmith.

An observant and energetic leader – a Botha or a De Wet – would immediately have used this opportunity to pursue and disperse the fleeing foot soldiers with his horsemen. This would have meant the end of the British opposition in Natal and the path to the sea would have been open. Unfortunately, Joubert was not that kind of leader. He allowed the British to return unhindered to Ladysmith where they immediately began to entrench themselves.

The siege of Ladysmith

The lost chance to annihilate White's troops soon came home to roost. Joubert did not want to attack the British in their fortified positions because he was afraid that this would claim too many lives. It was therefore decided in a council of war that Ladysmith would be besieged. The old tradition from the days of the wars against the Africans, namely to besiege the enemy by starving them out and forcing them to surrender was being used here in the war against the British.

The decision to besiege Ladysmith was fatal to the republican cause. Several thousand burghers who could have been used for other campaigns in Natal were now involved in a useless siege. The limited fighting capacity of the two republics was split without there being the least advantage from the exercise. The siege of Ladysmith simply helped to bring the republican offensive in Natal to a standstill, because after the British had

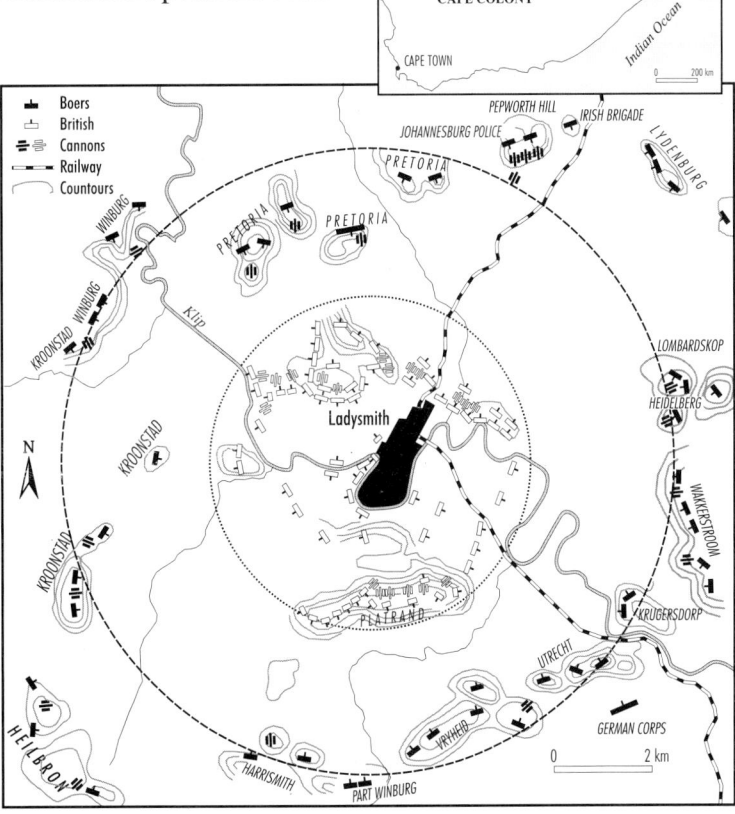

The siege of Ladysmith, 1899–1900

The siege of Ladysmith

landed reinforcements at Durban, the Boers could no longer achieve their goal of penetrating through to the coast.

The journey to Estcourt

It might still have been possible to occupy most of Natal if prompt action had been taken after the decision to besiege Ladysmith, because there were many opportunities for mobile mounted commandos to penetrate deep into enemy territory. But this chance was not utilised and instead all the commandos simply lingered around in the Ladysmith area. A full week passed before Colenso, on the Tugela River, was occupied on 8 November.

The best part of another week passed before Joubert decided on 13 November to move deeper into Natal with a force of between 3 000 and 4 000 men. This force was hopelessly too small for the conquest of Natal.

While the commandos delayed pointlessly at Ladysmith, trying to force the garrison to surrender, new troops landed in Durban and immediately marched north. More than 5 000 men under the leadership of General Barton and General Hildyard took up positions at Mooi River and Estcourt, hoping to protect Pietermaritzburg from an enemy attack.

The British defenders in Natal were thus stronger than the republican forces that were approaching which immediately meant that the scale had tipped in favour of the British.

On their southward journey Joubert's force derailed an armoured train near Chieveley station and captured a number of British soldiers. Among them was a journalist, Winston Churchill, who managed to escape after several weeks and joined the British forces again. He later became a famous statesman.

After this success, the republican troops continued on their journey south, but they still had to reckon with the British forces at Estcourt and Mooi River. It soon became clear that the numerical paucity of the commandos was inadequate to defeat the British force and break through to Pietermaritzburg and Durban. The ultra-cautious Joubert came to this conclusion after a nocturnal clash on 22 November at Willow Grange near Estcourt had ended inconclusively. He therefore decided to retreat to the Ladysmith area.

Thus any small measure of hope that the Boers might still reach the sea after the decision to besiege Ladysmith now also faded completely. The republican offensive in Natal had ground to a halt. The reasons for this were:

  (1) the mistake that had been made at Dundee in allowing the British to escape;
  (2) the delay in pursuing and dispersing the British forces after the victory at Modderspruit and Nicholson's Nek and the decision to besiege Ladysmith; and
  (3) the hesitation before moving deeper into Natal after the decision to besiege Ladysmith.

On the way back from Estcourt, Joubert was seriously injured in a fall and handed over control of the commandos to Botha. Botha, who could so easily have made a success of the offensive if he had been in command from the beginning, was forced to take up defensive positions on the

29

northern bank of the Tugela River at Colenso to prevent the British forces, which were now being continually reinforced, from penetrating through to Ladysmith.

THE WESTERN FRONT

The siege of Mafeking

When war broke out a small British force under the command of Colonel R.S.S. Baden-Powell was already stationed in Mafeking. This force was connected by rail to another force which was in Kimberley. The leader of the Kimberley troops was Colonel R.G. Kekewich. The Transvalers were to attack Mafeking, while the original plan was that the Free Staters should move out alone against Kimberley.

The Transvaal commandos which were going to operate on the western front were under the leadership of General P.A. Cronjé with General J.H. de la Rey as second in command. In many ways Cronjé contrasted strikingly with Joubert. He had true fighting spirit and challenged the enemy fearlessly, showing them scant regard. He was however also stubborn by nature and would never accept good advice and it was these latter characteristics that eventually led to his downfall.

Cronjé's first task was to cut off the railway link between Mafeking and Kimberley. This led to the first clash of the war on 12 October. A commando came to blows with an armoured train, derailed it and captured a number of enemy troops.

A Long Tom-cannon

It would have been reasonably easy for Cronjé to defeat Baden-Powell's small force at Mafeking by storming it with his mounted commandos, but he chose instead to besiege the town. His decision was apparently influenced by his experiences in the First War of Independence when he had besieged Potchefstroom and forced the garrison to surrender.

The siege of Mafeking

The decision to besiege Mafeking was a grave mistake because not only were a considerable number of burghers kept there needlessly, but Baden-Powell was determined to endure every hardship rather than surrender. By keeping a number of Boer commandos occupied around Mafeking Baden-Powell did the British cause a great service, because after some weeks the situation on the western front looked far less rosy for the two republics.

The siege of Kimberley

The siege of Kimberley was another serious error. If the Free State commandos had been under a determined commander, it would have been reasonably easy to attack the town successfully. Once again the Boers chose to besiege it instead and so more commandos were doomed to aimless inactivity despite the fact that they were needed elsewhere.

Instead these commandos could have penetrated deep into the Cape Colony and have shifted the theatre of war as far away from the borders of the republics as possible. The decision to besiege Kimberley and the

31

hesitation in taking decisive action meant that all the opportunities that had arisen were now lost. The commandos remained close to the Free State border and did not even occupy the bridge over the Orange River. This eventually gave the British forces an advantage which they subsequently put to very good use.

THE CAPE FRONT

Colesberg

Because the British were not fully organised to send enough troops to South Africa when war was declared on 11 October, they did not have a strong force ready to send to the region south of the Orange River. This was significant because in this part of the Cape Colony there were important railway junctions at De Aar and Noupoort. In addition, the residents of these districts were sympathetic to the Boer cause.

The republican forces could therefore have gained an important advantage with an invasion over the Orange River into the Cape. Had they acted swiftly, it would have been possible to penetrate deep into the Cape Colony, far from the borders of the republics, and to attack the British forces that had landed at one of the harbours. Here indeed was a golden opportunity for mobile commandos who were prepared to act fast.

But the republican forces did not capitalise on any of these opportunities. Nowhere else did the commandos show such lethargy as they did in the Cape Colony.

The advance took place along two routes. The first was via Colesberg, a small town in the Cape Colony situated a few kilometres from the Orange River. The first three weeks of the war passed without a single commando crossing the river.

Only on 1 November — after a Transvaal commando under General H.Schoeman came to reinforce the Free Staters — was Norvalspont occupied. Such slow progress was made that it was not until 14 November that Colesberg was occupied. Thereafter the commandos made practically no more headway.

There was not even a single attempt to occupy Noupoort and De Aar, so the railway remained in British hands. This proved to be an invaluable advantage, particularly when they began their offensive.

Stormberg

The republicans' second invasion into the Cape Colony was made via Aliwal North, Venterstad and Burgersdorp. It was not until 13 November that a commando under Commandant Olivier crossed the Orange River at Aliwal North. Just as had been the case at Colesberg, here a considerable number of Cape Afrikaners joined the republican forces.

The whole advance now stalled and the commandos occupied Stormberg without moving any further into the Cape Colony. This gave the British the opportunity to concentrate a few regiments at Queenstown.

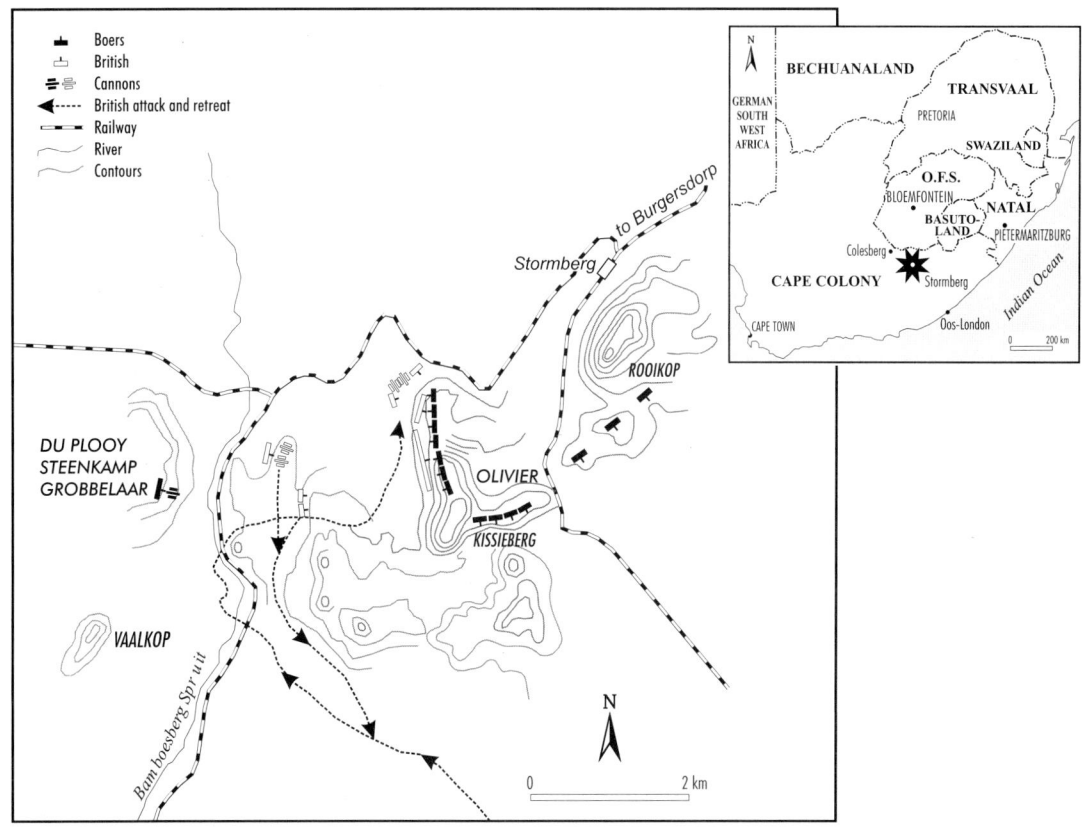

Stormberg, 10 December 1899

REASONS FOR THE FAILURE
OF THE REPUBLICAN OFFENSIVE

Within six weeks of the beginning of the war the republican offensive had ground to a halt. The opportunities that had arisen to take the war deep into enemy territory and even perhaps to reach the sea had been squandered. Thereby any chance of winning the war was irrevocably lost. The main reason for the failure of the offensive is easily summarised: the military leaders of the two republics were simply not equal to the task.

At the outbreak of the war the republican forces had no really capable leaders. They did not have the pluck and initiative to make good use of the opportunities presented to them. Furthermore they had no clear plan of action. To make a success of the offensive, the commandos should have used their mobility. They should have covered long distances in the shortest possible time. Later in the war these tactics were in fact used, but in the opening months the republican forces were certainly not characterised by their mobility.

The weak leadership also affected the morale of the burghers. Good officers would have been able to maintain a measure of discipline as was the case later in the war. Initially, however, the discipline was very poor and this also contributed to the failure of the offensive.

CHAPTER III
THE FAILURE OF THE FIRST BRITISH OFFENSIVE

While the republican forces were moving lethargically ahead in late October and the first few weeks of November, the first reinforcements of thousands of soldiers arrived in Cape Town from Britain. They were under the leadership of General Redvers Buller who was to be in supreme command of all the British forces in South Africa. The original strategy was that Buller would first go to the northern part of the Cape Colony, destroy the weak republican forces there, and then he would push on to Bloemfontein with the railway ensuring a constant supply of the necessary provisions.

This was undoubtedly a sound plan and Buller would have met with little resistance if he had implemented it. Indeed, if he had succeeded he would probably have caused a complete turn-about of fortunes in the war.

While Buller was in Cape Town making his preparations, the news that came in from Natal about White's defeat on 30 October grew progressively worse. The British were concerned that the republican forces might succeed in breaking through to Durban. It was this possibility that made Buller decide to make substantial alterations to his original plan.

The first division of troops which arrived was immediately sent to Natal. These were the men who checked the republican forces at Estcourt and who undoubtedly saved Natal from another attack. But Buller was to go even further. He divided his force again. He decided to take personal command of the largest part and to advance into Natal to drive the commandos back and relieve Ladysmith.

Two smaller divisions were also active in the Cape Colony. The first, under the leadership of General Lord Metheun, was to cross the Orange River and relieve Kimberley. The second, with General W.F. Gatacre in command, landed in East London and was sent to Queenstown. Its task was to drive the Boer forces out of the Stormberg Mountains. With the arrival of so many thousands of troops, the British were able to take the initiative and go on the attack, but the deviation from their original plan and the dispersal of their forces were to cost them dearly.

THE NATAL FRONT

Buller in Natal

After he had divided the British force into three, Buller moved to Natal with the largest part, arriving on 25 November — just at the precise time that Joubert's commandos were returning from Estcourt to take up their positions at Colenso. In Natal there was now a British army of more than 19 000 men who were ready to relieve Ladysmith and drive back the republicans.

Against this strong force that was drawn up near the Tugela River, Botha could only muster about 5 000 men. The rest of the republican forces were still busy with the fruitless, senseless siege of Ladysmith. Botha was a born military leader and in the available time he made absolutely sure that there were formidable entrenchments on the ridges along the banks of the Tugela. But Botha realised that his position had one weakness, although at the time the British were unaware of this.

Near Colenso the Tugela River takes a sharp turn towards the north. Hlangwane Hill (also called Bosrant) lies in this curve. If the British were to take possession of the hill they would have been able, with their heavy fire power, to bombard all the republican trenches on the opposite side and make their position untenable. Botha was thus forced to occupy this hill as well and this meant that part of his force had to be stationed on the southern bank of the Tugela.

Colenso

Shortly after Buller's arrival in Durban he advanced northwards at the head of the force that would attempt to relieve Ladysmith.

Buller decided that 15 December would be the memorable day on which he would drive Botha out of his entrenchments at Colenso and make a

Arrival of the first British prisoners of war in Pretoria

triumphant entry into Ladysmith. His battle plan was that four columns would cross the Tugela to attack the enemy. One column would form the left wing, while two others, supported by artillery, would form the main force on either side of the railway and would cross the river at Colenso. The fourth column on the right wing was assigned the task of capturing Hlangwane Hill.

The sun was barely up that morning when the Boers in their trenches saw the deployment of the British forces. Quiet and composed, they waited for the enemy to come within reach of their mausers. These men from the Swaziland Police and the commandos from Ermelo, Standerton, Middelburg, Boksburg, Heidelberg, Vryheid, Krugersdorp and Wakkerstroom were also emotionally ready: their fighting spirit was mirrored in their eyes. They had strict orders not to fire a single shot until Botha gave the signal to do so. Luckily, the burghers had nerves of steel and they remained calm and unruffled. With every passing moment the enemy foot soldiers came closer to the river and artillery fire was spurting down into the republican trenches. But still there was no Boer reaction, giving Buller the impression that his enemy had abandoned its position. Shortly after 6:30 the British left wing was next to the Tugela.

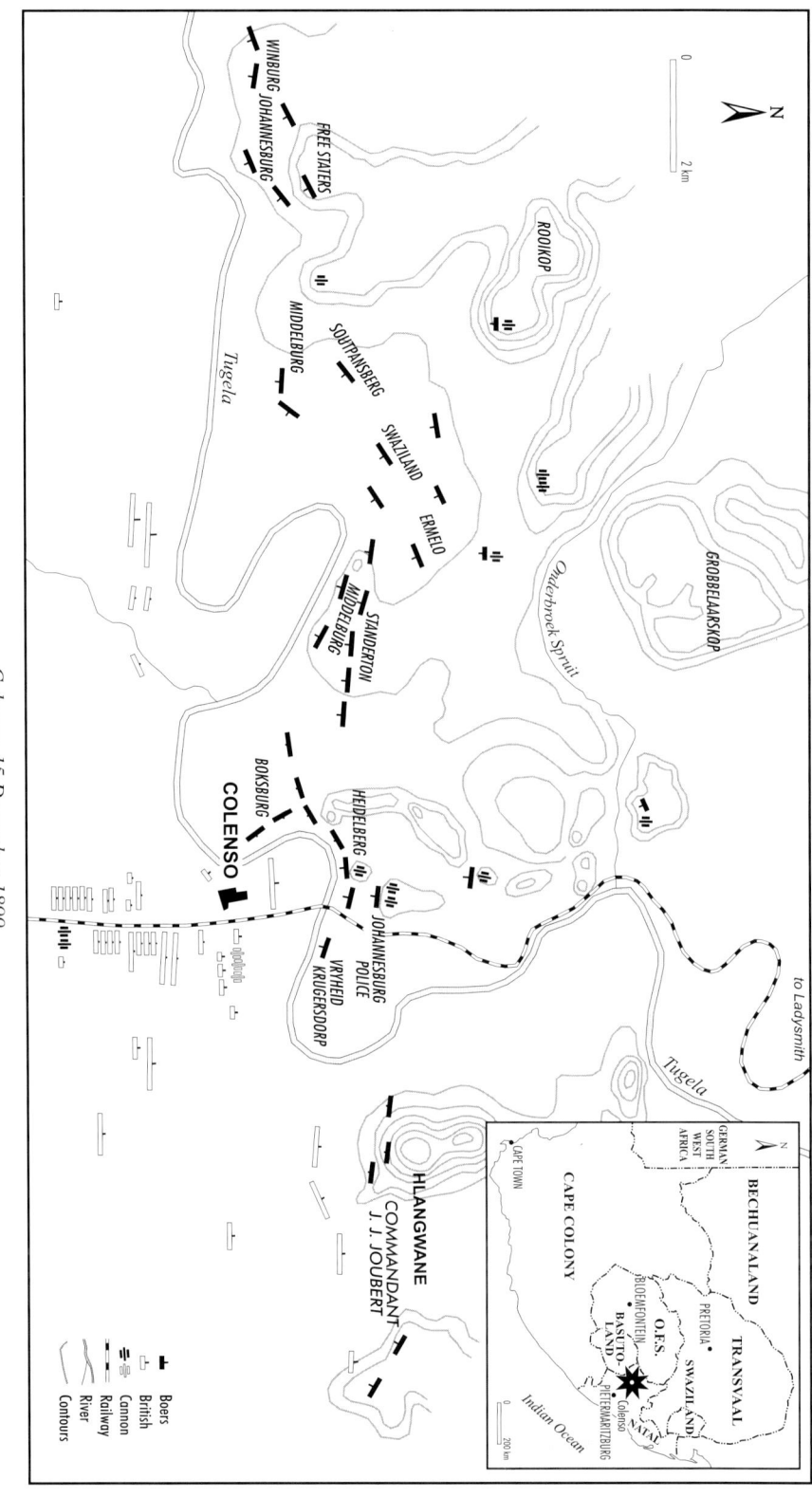

Colenso, 15 December 1899

Suddenly a grenade from a Boer cannon exploded among the soldiers. This was Botha's signal for the shooting to begin. Along the entire line there was now a roar as gunfire rained down on the enemy. The British were unable to withstand this murderous fire and soon the ground was strewn with the dead and wounded. The terrain gave the British soldiers no cover at all and they remained completely exposed to the Boer fire.

By contrast, there was simply no sign of the Boers. In their trenches they were completely hidden. Close to Colenso the British gunners ventured out with their cannons almost to the river's edge and were all simply mown down. Brave attempts were made to rescue the cannons, but they were unsuccessful because of the accurate fire from the other side of the river.

Buller eventually realised that he was needlessly sacrificing the lives of his men. He had suffered a major defeat and by eleven o'clock he gave the order that his columns should retreat. More than a thousand British soldiers had been killed or wounded and in addition ten valuable cannons had been left in the hands of the Boers. On the republican side only six men had died and 22 had been wounded.

The first attempt to relieve Ladysmith had ended in a humiliating defeat for the British.

Platrand

Even after the major encounter at Colenso, the siege of Ladysmith dragged on. This had a very negative effect on the morale of the burghers. Nowhere else did the lack of discipline become as apparent as right there around Ladysmith. The vigilance that is so crucial during wartime was also slackening. The British made full use of this on the night of 7 to 8 December when they damaged one of the big Creusot cannons, better known as Long Tom, so badly that it had to be sent to Pretoria to be repaired.

After the first British attempt to relieve Ladysmith, the republican command realised that it had become necessary to end the siege by forcing the garrison to surrender.

White's men had already entrenched themselves everywhere and to root them out would clearly be difficult. To the south of Ladysmith there is a long sloping hill known as Platrand. If Platrand could be captured, all the other British positions could then be attacked from the rear. Platrand was in other words the key to the conquest of Ladysmith. The British also realised this and had therefore fortified the hill very securely.

Early in January 1900 the republican commanders decided that Platrand should be captured by means of a swift charge. In the early morning of 6 January a large number of burghers crept very silently up the sides of the hill. Immediately fierce fighting broke out which raged on until the afternoon.

The burghers were successful in taking a number of British trenches, but the soldiers defended the others stubbornly and were also fortunate enough to receive reinforcements, whereas no additional support turned up for the republican forces. Both sides suffered heavy losses and finally, when it seemed clear that they could not take Platrand, the republicans had to retreat.

White continued to hold out in Ladysmith until the town was relieved nearly two months later.

British troops at Spioenkop

Spioenkop

In the next chapter it will be shown that the defeat of the British forces at Colenso led to Buller being replaced as supreme commander of the British forces in South Africa.

Before his successor arrived, Buller was keen to make another attempt to break through to Ladysmith. Early in January 1900 he again received thousands of reinforcements. This time Buller was very wary not to be caught up against the Colenso trenches.

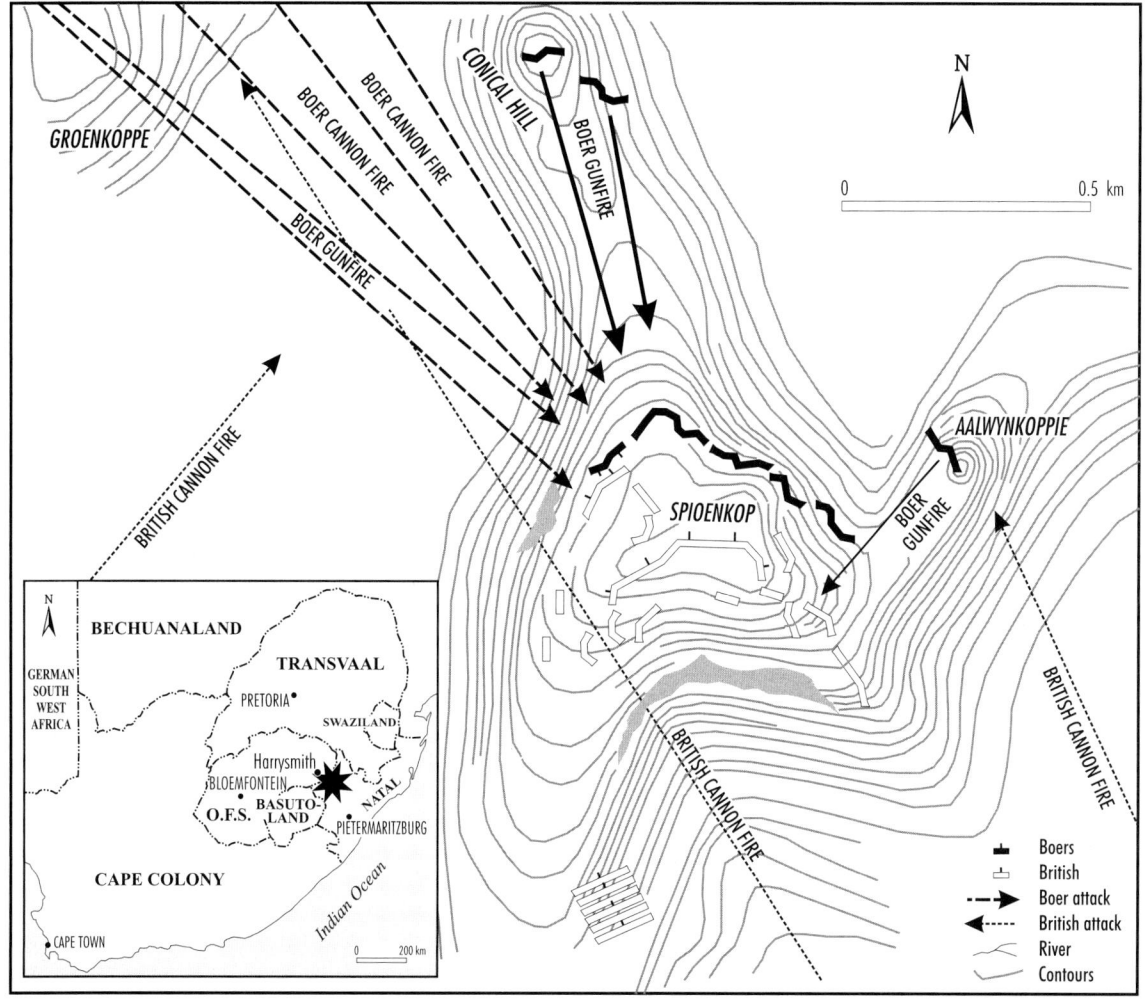

Spioenkop, 24 January 1900

He decided to cross the Tugela a few kilometres from Colenso and skirt around the right flank of the republican forces. If he succeeded in doing this, the way through to Ladysmith would be open for him.

The first British troops moved into position on 10 January and occupied a drift on the Tugela River. But Buller was extremely tardy and one day after another passed without much progress being made. This also gave Botha the opportunity to send some of his commandos to the west to block the British route. Meanwhile, a sizeable number of British troops began to cross the Tugela without meeting much Boer opposition. For a few days sporadic skirmishes took place there without either side gaining much advantage. On 22 January the British army command decided that Spioenkop should be occupied by a strong force, because from the top of this high hill it would be possible to bombard the republican trenches with cannon fire. The commandos were holding Spioenkop with only a very weak defence and when the British troops came up the sides of the hill during the night of 23 to 24 January, they reached the summit without any opposition.

The handful of burghers who were there immediately took to their heels and the British promptly began to entrench themselves.

When Botha discovered on the morning of 24 January what had happened during the night, he immediately gave the order that Spioenkop should be recaptured, and one of the most hotly contested battles of the war broke out. Just as had happened at Majuba and Nicholson's Nek, the burghers clambered up the sides of the hill almost unseen by the British.

Meanwhile the cannons of the State Artillery which was under the command of Major J.F. Wolmarans were sowing death and destruction on Spioenkop. The British casualties grew with every hour that passed and among those who were killed was General Woodgate who had been in command of the regiments that had ascended Spioenkop. When the burghers reached the summit, there was an absolute massacre of the British soldiers. Buller sent in reinforcements, but they soon met with the same fate as their comrades. For the British it was a blessed relief when the battle eventually had to be stopped at nightfall. Under cover of darkness they abandoned Spioenkop and retreated to the south of the Tugela. It was only on the following morning that Botha realised that once again he had triumphed against Buller. On the British side the toll was almost 2 000 men killed and wounded, while in contrast fewer than 200 burghers had met their death or been wounded in the battle.

The second attempt to relieve Ladysmith had also ended in a major defeat for the British.

Vaalkrans

Buller was forced to allow his soldiers a few weeks rest after this second heavy defeat. But when he had yet again received reinforcements, he decided to launch a new attempt to relieve Ladysmith. This time he thought he would try to reach his objective by crossing the Tugela at Vaalkrans, between Colenso and Spioenkop, so on 5 February his troops crossed the river again and occupied one or two hills on the northern side. The British movements were again so painfully slow that Botha was given more than enough time to draw up a number of commandos at the threatened point and so obstruct the enemy's path. The opposition was of such a nature that Buller could well have suffered another Spioenkop and he did not relish this idea at all. On 8 February he gave the order to withdraw his troops.

This third attempt to relieve Ladysmith thus also ended in failure for the British.

THE WESTERN FRONT

Methuen on the western front

While he was delayed in Cape Town, Buller had decided to send Methuen to the north with a force of more than 8 500 men. His orders were to relieve Kimberley. Methuen would also receive reinforcements from time to time.

Thanks to the fact that the republican forces did not make use of the opportunity to invade deep into the Cape Colony, Methuen was able to send his troops by rail as far as the Orange River. He also thought it best to move along the railway line to Kimberley because it would be so much easier to bring in military supplies.

Belmont

Against Methuen's force the republicans could initially muster only 2 500 men because the others were involved in the siege of Kimberley. Here too, a senseless siege thus led to a serious splintering of the republican forces. The commandos who were sent to block Methuen's path were under the orders of Commandant J. Prinsloo.

The first clash between the two forces took place on 23 November at Belmont station. As was often the case in the beginning of the war, the Boers left it to the British to go on the attack. The Boer forces took up their positions in a series of ridges and waited there for the enemy. Methuen immediately ordered his men to launch a frontal attack. Although they suffered heavy losses, the British soldiers were undaunted and fought back, driving their opponents from one position after another. After a few hours they took possession of all the ridges and the republican forces had to retreat to the north.

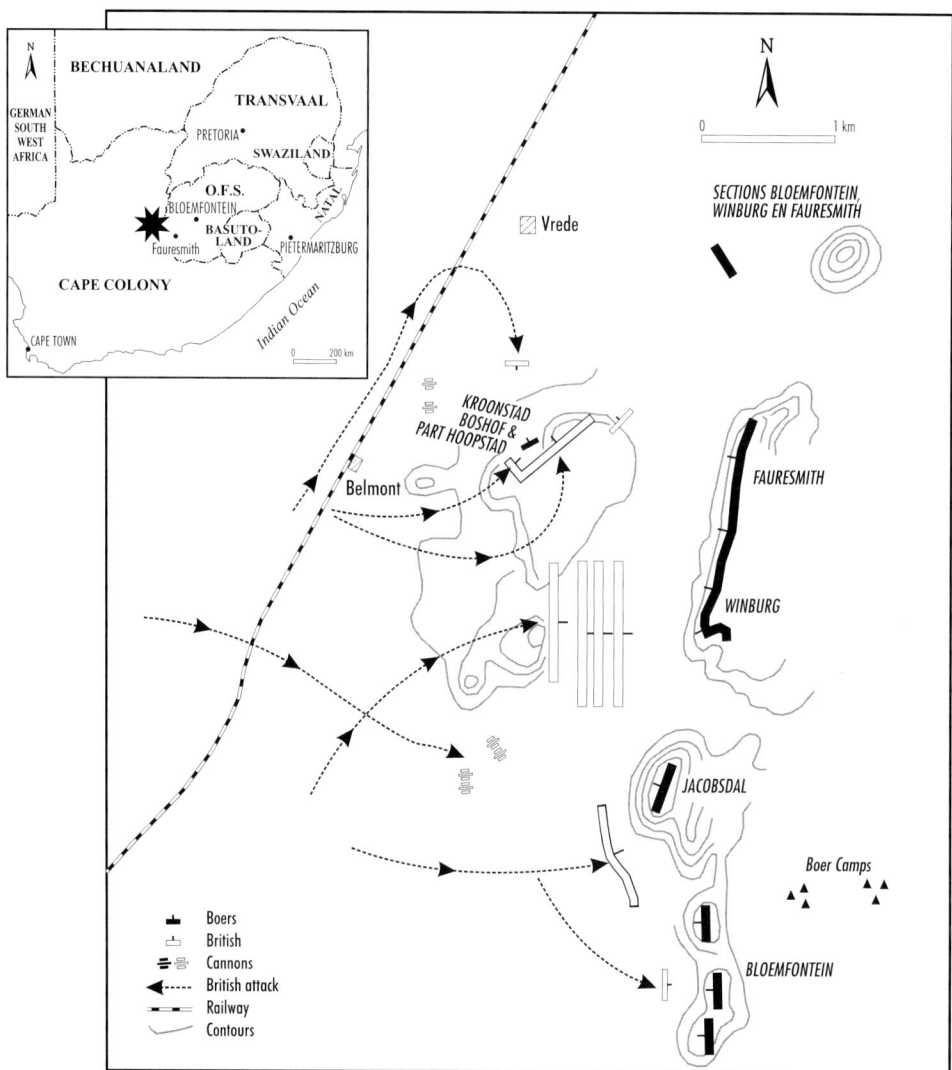

Belmont, 23 November 1899

Graspan

The victory at Belmont meant only a territorial gain for Methuen. He was able to move a number of kilometres nearer to Kimberley, but the republican forces still stood between him and his objective.

44

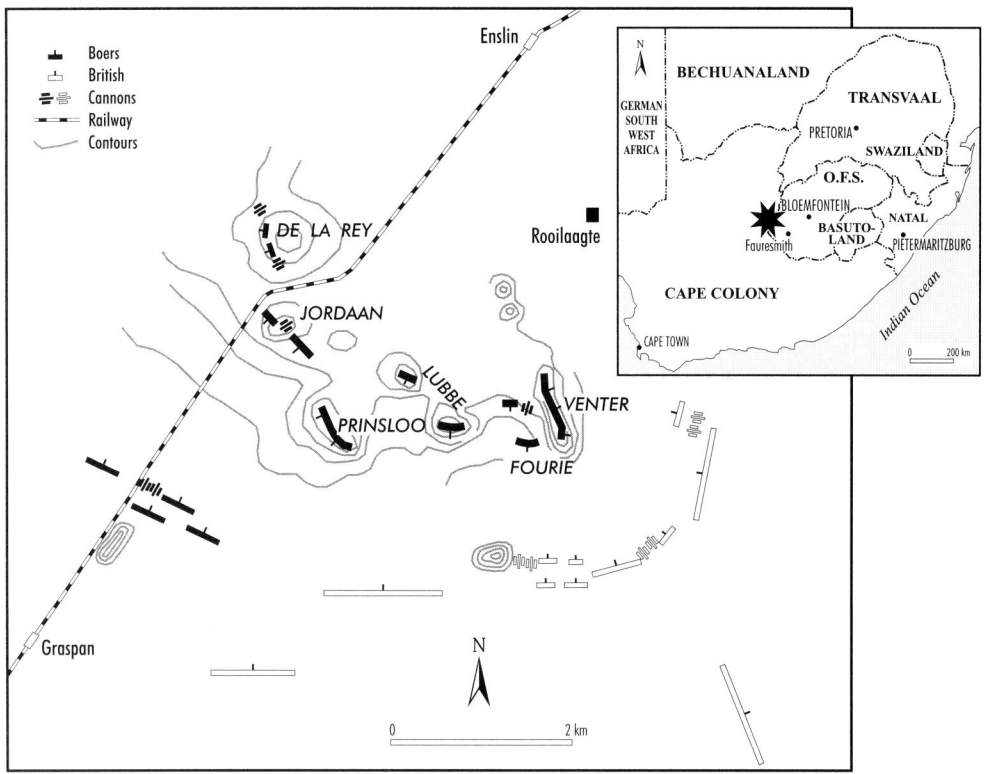

Graspan, 25 November 1899

Strengthened by the addition of a few commandos that had come from Kimberley with De la Rey, the republican forces occupied new positions near the railway at Graspan. As before, they positioned themselves in some ridges, where they were attacked again by the British on 25 November.

This time Methuen's initial tactics were to use his artillery to fire fiercely onto the republican position. The exploding grenades among the granite rocks made conditions very difficult for the commandos and when the British infantry went on the attack a few hours later, the Boer forces had to yield once again.

Modder River

It was disheartening for the republican forces that within the space of a few days they had suffered a second defeat. Nevertheless they were fortunate enough to be strengthened by a few thousand men who had come with Cronjé from Mafeking. Cronjé assumed the command and

45

General Piet Cronjé

decided to take up a new position on the banks of the Modder River. This was done under pressure from De la Rey who, after the experience at Graspan, decided that the tactic of taking a stand on stony ridges was unwise because the artillery fire could cause heavy losses. Instead, the burghers had to find cover in ditches where the enemy would be unable to see them.

With the Boers now in the natural trenches that they had selected, Methuen attacked them for the third time on 28 November. On this occasion, the burghers on the river bank maintained their furious fire on the enemy and inflicted such grave losses that it initially looked as if Methuen was going to meet with a heavy defeat. But after the battle had raged for a few hours, the day was saved for Methuen by his left wing which discovered a weak point in the Boer defences. These soldiers succeeded in crossing the river which gave Methuen the opportunity to send more of his regiments across. Because Cronjé's forces now thought that they were not strong enough to drive the British back, some of the commandos began to desert their posts, forcing their commander to evacuate the battlefield just before sunset, without the British being aware of it.

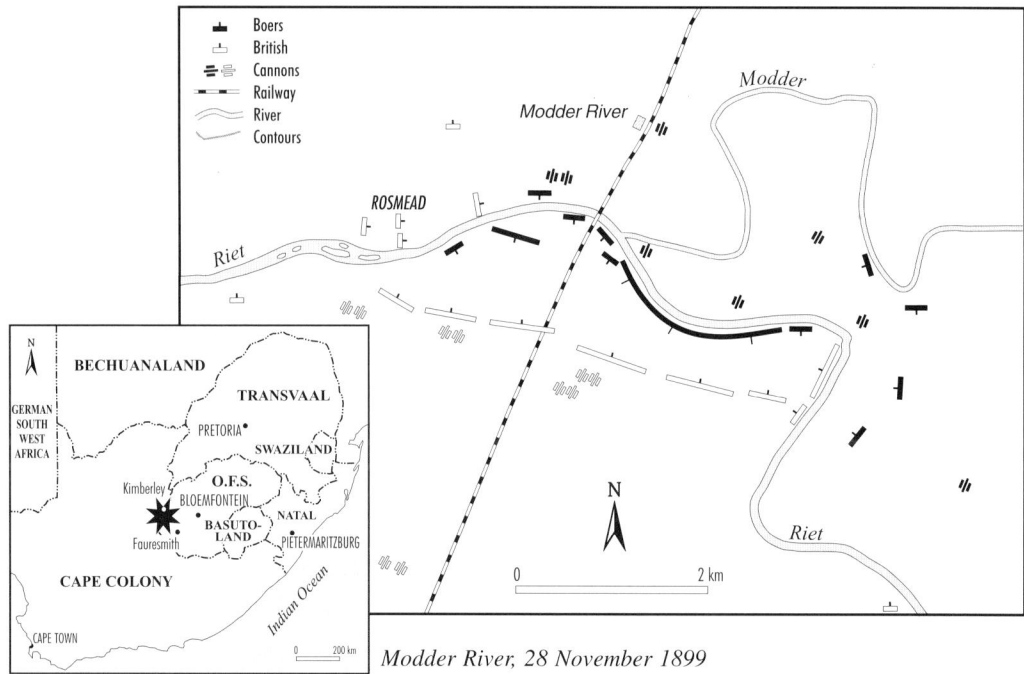

Modder River, 28 November 1899

46

The fact that the republican forces had deserted their excellent position was, according to De la Rey's subsequent statements, a serious error, because if they had stood firm they would have forced the enemy to fall back. In fact, poor discipline was the reason why the battle at the Modder River did not end in a clear victory for the Boers.

Magersfontein

Although the battle at Modder River meant that Methuen moved closer to Kimberley, the losses he had suffered were so serious that he had to wait for reinforcements before he felt confident enough to tackle the opposition again. The republican forces used the time this gave them to good advantage, and dug a series of trenches below the ridges of Magersfontein. Here the burghers awaited the arrival of the enemy. Once he had received his reinforcements, Methuen began to bombard the ridges mercilessly with his heavy cannons. This gave the Boers very little trouble because in their trenches they were completely protected from the exploding shells.

On 10 December Methuen at last decided that the time was ripe to launch his fourth attack on the republican forces. By midnight a number of regiments — most of them Scottish — under the command of Major-General Wauchope, set off to attack the Boer trenches at daybreak.

The battle at Magersfontein

47

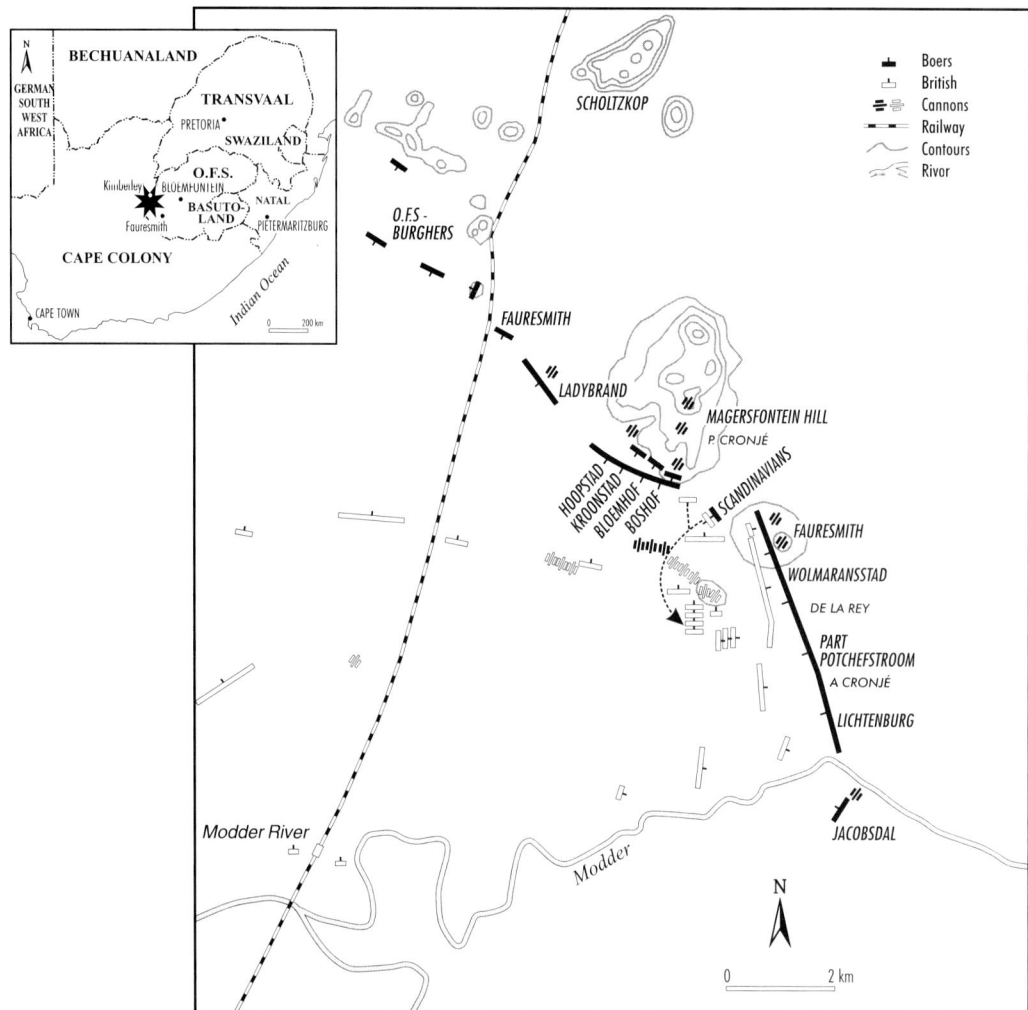

Magersfontein, 11 December 1899

Because it was raining and still dark, the soldiers found it difficult to maintain their formations. There was thus even at this early stage, a certain amount of confusion in the British ranks.

The sound of many thousands of pairs of feet on the veld, coming ever nearer, alerted the burghers. Quiet and composed, they awaited the moment when it would be light enough to see the enemy and open fire on them. By four o'clock, in the early dawn of 11 December, the darkness slowly lifted. Suddenly the men who had sharp eyes saw the British a hundred paces away and instantly fire began to blaze from the mausers.

The battle of Magersfontein had begun. One of the first men to perish was Wauchope and his death immediately caused great disarray. Shortly after the fighting had begun, the sun came up and in the clear light of day the Scots with their picturesque, kilted military uniforms were easy targets for the sharpshooters. In addition, the veld provided very little cover and the number of dead and wounded increased rapidly. The day was very hot and it was torture to lie there in the baking sun — especially for those who had been wounded and to whom very little assistance could be given.

Cronjé was everywhere. He issued orders and saw to it that the enemy was given no chance to break through. His opposite number, Methuen, followed the progress of the battle from a nearby koppie, and by four in the afternoon he eventually had to admit that he had suffered a major defeat. It was then difficult to persuade his demoralised soldiers to get back out of the Boer firing line. Methuen had lost almost a thousand men in his fruitless attack on Magersfontein.

In comparison the Boer losses were mild. The small Scandinavian Corps, which had not been fighting from a trench and had come to blows with a strong enemy division early in the battle, was almost completely wiped out.

After his defeat, Methuen decided provisionally that he would not embark on any more attempts to relieve Kimberley. A silence, which was not to be broken until February 1900, descended upon the western front.

THE CAPE FRONT

Stormberg

In December 1899 and January 1900 there were only a few minor skirmishes in the Colesberg region. The forces facing one another here were so small that there were no serious encounters.

The situation was different at Stormberg. In the most northerly districts of the Cape Colony the majority of Afrikaners sympathised with the republican cause and many of them joined the commandos. This caused some consternation among the British authorities and it was felt that this spirit of rebellion could only be dealt a death blow if the republican forces were made to suffer a humiliating defeat.

It was with this in mind that Gatacre decided to surprise the commandos that had positioned themselves on Stormberg Mountain, and to drive them back. On the night of 9 December, with this goal in sight, he set off from Molteno where his troops had been drawn up. His plan was to

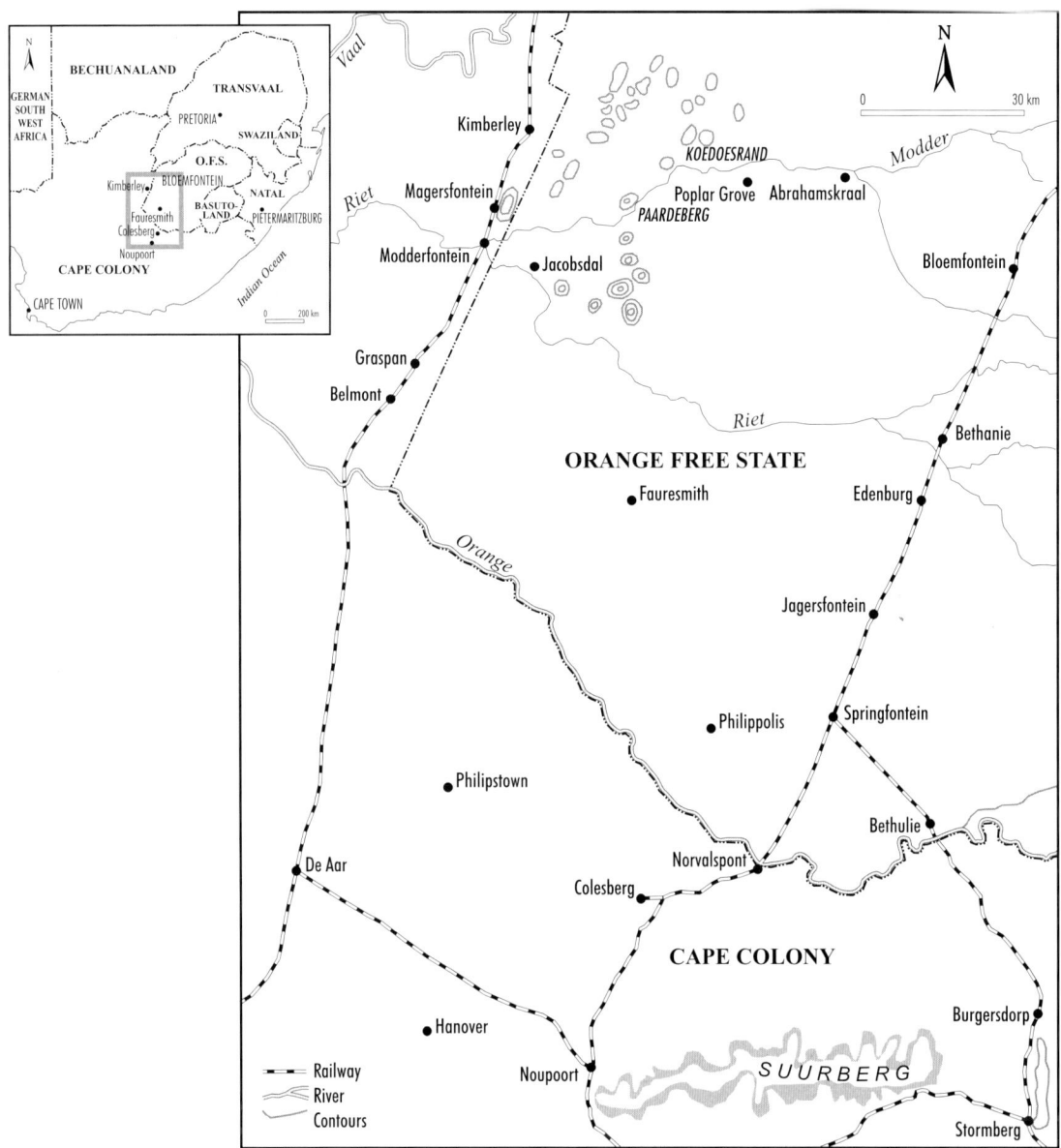

The Southern front, 1899–1900

make a surprise atttack on the Boers early the next morning. But from the outset things went awry. The British lost their way in the darkness and at daybreak on the morning of 10 December, they were not at all sure where they were.

They were in fact very close to the commandos that had taken up their positions on the summit of Stormberg Mountain. The burghers in these commandos were from Smithfield, Bethulie and Rouxville and were under Commandant Olivier. Immediately after the guards had spotted the first British soldiers in the dim light, they began to fire. This instantly woke the other burghers and within a few minutes hectic gunfire rained down on the enemy at the foot of the mountain. The British had wanted to surprise the Boers, but had themselves been caught unawares by this unexpected gunfire, and there was soon great confusion in their ranks.

The British could see practically nothing of the Boers, but they themselves were clearly visible to their opponents. Gatacre tried to bring his artillery into action so that the infantry could go on the attack, but even the cannon fire had little effect on the burghers and after a few hours the British had to halt the attack and retreat.

Gatacre's losses at Stormberg were in excess of 600 men killed, wounded and taken prisoner.

REASONS FOR THE FAILURE
OF THE BRITISH OFFENSIVE

In December 1899 the number of British soldiers on the various fronts already exceeded the number of burghers. And yet the British offensive had failed on all fronts and had suffered three heavy defeats within a single week – Stormberg on 10 December, Magersfontein on 11 December and Colenso on 15 December. To what can the failure of this first British offensive be attributed?

The answer to this question is clear. It was the inefficiency of the most senior British commanders. The republican offensive had also failed because of the fact that their military leaders were unequal to their task. Similarly, the fate of the British offensive was determined by incompetent men like Buller, Methuen and Gatacre. Buller in particular made a serious error when he decided to divide the British forces. As has already been noted, the numerical distribution to the various fronts can also be seriously questioned.

The inefficiency of the British commanders was most apparent on the battlefield. They knew only one kind of assault: a frontal attack. They sent their soldiers directly towards the Boer positions, making matters far easier for the republican forces. In the fortifications that they could prepare beforehand, the burghers could await the enemy attacks in complete safety. They had always understood the art of making themselves well nigh invisible to their opponents, while the enemy as it were, came marching right into the path of the mausers. Under such circumstances the British commanders were simply sending their soldiers into the jaws of death.

The British themselves were thus responsible to a considerable degree for the failure of their offensive.

CHAPTER IV
THE SECOND
BRITISH OFFENSIVE SUCCEEDS

The British reaction

Suffering three grave defeats in a single week had a huge emotional impact on the British people. Seldom before had Britain's prestige in the eyes of the world taken such a knock as it did after this setback in South Africa. The Christmas of 1899 was celebrated in a very sombre mood in Britain. The general feeling was that a far greater effort would have to be made and a new offensive should be launched. It was this realisation that made the British government decide to take two strategic steps. The first was to send another large body of soldiers to South Africa once again. This meant that the numerical strength of the British forces would be increased to more than 200 000. The second step was to appoint Lord Roberts as commander-in-chief in Buller's place. Roberts left Britain for South Africa at the end of December accompanied by Lord Kitchener as his chief of staff.

These two men arrived in Cape Town in January 1900. They had decided on a brand new strategy. Their first objective would be to relieve Kimberley and thereafter they would march to Bloemfontein with a very large force. They had learnt from their previous mistakes. Roberts and Kitchener would not resort to frontal attacks unless these were absolutely necessary. Using their cavalry, they would now use the ploy of trying to skirt around the wings of the opposition. The fear of being encircled had often in the past forced the commandos to desert their positions and retreat. Under Roberts and Kitchener the British army would now gain a mobility that it had not previously possessed.

Whereas Buller had made use of the old military tactics at Spioenkop and Vaalkrans, Roberts and Kitchener now made careful preparations for their proposed new strategy. More than 30 000 men were stationed in readiness at Modder River, and at the beginning of February the two generals set off to join them. The new British offensive can be conveniently divided into three phases. The first ends with the occupation of

Bloemfontein and the relief of Ladysmith, while the second phase closes with the occupation of Pretoria. Britain's occupation of the major portion of the Transvaal and Free State, and Kitchener's takeover of control from Roberts, mark the end of the third phase. A separate chapter will be devoted to each of these phases.

THE WESTERN FRONT

The relief of Kimberley

After the battle of Magersfontein, Cronjé's forces had a period of complete inactivity. While the British army was being reinforced on an almost daily basis, the Boers quite simply did nothing. Many of their wagons started arriving at the front, some of them complete with wives and children. This and the fact that a considerable number of burghers no longer owned horses meant that the mobility of the republican forces was seriously impaired. It can in fact be claimed that while the British forces were being strengthened, the republican forces were deteriorating.

This situation was a source of grave concern to a man like De Wet. Steyn had appointed him as a general on 7 December and had sent him to the western front. De Wet was of the opinion that the commandos should be kept highly active and that the enemy should hardly be allowed to relax for a single moment. They should be constantly harassed and their lines of communication should be cut off by commandos that could move around very rapidly.

De Wet asked Cronjé's permission to take this approach, but Cronjé refused. Because the British wanted to begin their campaign only when they had an overwhelmingly superior force, it was not until the middle of February that any serious conflict took place on the western front.

To relieve Kimberley, Roberts decided to use his cavalry which was placed under the orders of General French. The cavalry would move around Cronjé's left wing and march in an arc towards Kimberley. They would be closely followed by a strong force of foot soldiers that had to occupy Jacobsdal and destroy Cronjé's communications. Then his entire force could be destroyed.

Roberts's strategy was a brilliant success. On 15 February French and his men rode into Kimberley and the commandos had to retreat to the north hastily. The British infantry advanced in their thousands into the Free State and threatened to cut off the republican forces.

Paardeberg

The new British offensive came as a complete surprise to Cronjé. His position at Magersfontein was now indefensible and he was forced to evacuate it as quickly as circumstances allowed. Because his burghers were accompanied by hundreds of wagons, the retreat was very slow. Furthermore, he could only take a route that would provide enough water for the people and their animals, which meant that he had to follow the

The battle of Paardeberg

Modder River and thread his way through the British lines. The enemy also had very little trouble in catching up with Cronjé. When the news reached French that Cronjé was moving slowly along the Modder River, he and his horsemen left Kimberley and rode off in a northerly direction to cut him off. French was one of the most capable British commanders, and would certainly have succeeded, but he was also assisted by Cronjé himself who was reluctant to leave his cumbersome wagon train behind. Had he been prepared to do so and to move off quickly with all his mounted troops, they would easily have been able to escape the threat of encirclement

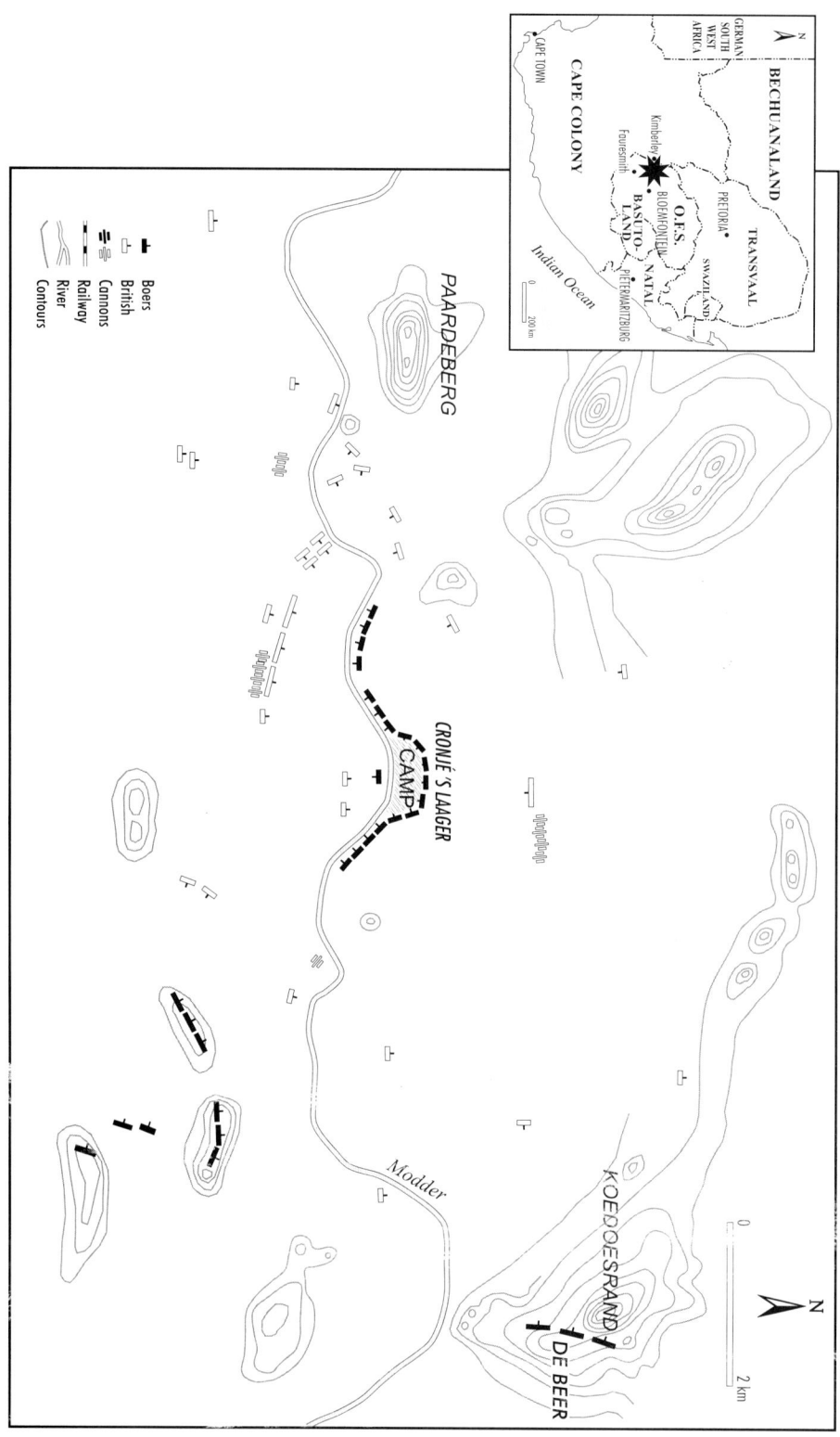

Paardeberg, February 1900

by the enemy. But Cronjé refused to do this. Behind him the British infantry was bearing down on him in their thousands and ahead, French's cavalry urged on their now-tiring horses to reach Koedoesdrif, a ford over the Modder River, before the ponderous Boer force could get there.

When Cronjé prepared to cross the river at a point close to Paardeberg on the afternoon of 17 February, he discovered that he had been cut off. He was now encircled on every side by British troops.

With such a huge force against him it was just a matter of how long Cronjé would be able to hold out. His burghers dug themselves into the banks of the Modder River and held on valiantly for ten days. Although their appalling conditions deteriorated daily, they made the enemy pay very dearly for their capture. Kitchener, who had initially taken over the command in the absence of Roberts, was made well aware of this. He wanted to claim the honour of forcing Cronjé to surrender and on 18 February he launched a heavy attack on the laager.

What resulted was perhaps predictable. The British were beaten back with dreadful losses and left behind on the battlefield more men killed and wounded than in any other battle of the war. Roberts arrived soon afterwards and had the satisfaction of launching an almost continuous retaliatory bombardment on the laager.

While Cronjé was trapped, De Wet was doing all he possibly could to release him from the British encirclement. De Wet came to the fore at this stage and was to remain a leading figure right until the end of the war. He had already come to the realisation that if he moved faster than the British forces he could very easily attack them from the rear and inflict great damage. De Wet now began to adopt this strategy. While the British forces were advancing into the Free State, he used the small force that he had at his disposal to slip around behind them and seize the soldiers' food supplies. The fact that Roberts preferred to let his soldiers go hungry rather than to halt the attack on Cronjé was proof enough that De Wet's brave actions had succeeded in hampering the British advance.

De Wet did his utmost to save Cronjé. When he had received reinforcements, he attacked the British force around Cronjé at a specific point and opened an escape route for Cronjé. If Cronjé had been prepared to leave his wagons behind, it would have been possible for him to escape from behind, but he failed to use the opportunity because not all his

Danie Theron

subordinates would agree. Even when De Wet helped the well-known Captain Danie Theron slip through the British lines with the suggestion that Cronjé should try to fight his way out while De Wet gave him support from the outside, nothing happened. Eventually De Wet had no alternative but to leave, because the British were also threatening to surround his burghers.

Realistically, the encirclement of Cronjé could have had only one outcome. On the morning of 27 February, Majuba Day, Cronjé and more than 3 000 of his men surrendered to Roberts. Soon afterwards they were sent to St Helena Island in the Atlantic Ocean, where they were imprisoned until the end of the war.

Bloemfontein

Cronjé's surrender was a bitter blow to the republican forces. Firstly, it had a very demoralising effect on the morale of the burghers. They lost hope and began to doubt that they could ever win the war. Secondly, a substantial part of the commandos that had withstood the enemy so succesfully in Natal had to be sent to the western front to try to halt Roberts's march. It will be shown later what effect this had on the Natal front.

After his victory at Paardeberg, Roberts was able to continue his march to Bloemfontein. Between him and the Free State capital stood De Wet and his burghers. Although the Free Staters were to be strengthened by a number of Transvaal commandos under De la Rey, the British army was still far stronger, and Roberts was to make good use of this advantage. His strategy was to use his cavalry to encircle the wings of the commandos.

De Wet entrenched himself at Poplar Grove and waited for the British attack. But Roberts certainly did not plan to walk straight into the gunfire of the enemy as his predecessors had done. He simply sent out his cavalry to move around the left wing of the Boers and get behind them. The plan worked to perfection. The British horsemen were still executing the manoeuvre when the burghers took flight because they were terrified of being encircled. De Wet's attempts to stand firm were in vain. Roberts simply gained a bloodless victory.

Although he was forced into retreating, De Wet did not abandon the struggle. Together with De la Rey he took up new positions at Abrahamskraal, which is also on the Modder River. Here, on 10 March, Roberts went on the attack again.

Despite the fact that this time the burghers offered brave resistance, the enemy had such an overwhelming numerical advantage that the Boers had to evacuate their positions again. On 13 March Roberts's troops marched into Bloemfontein unchallenged. Steyn and the Free State government had already left the previous day for Kroonstad.

After a struggle lasting more than a month the British forces were exhausted and needed to rest, so Roberts decided to delay in Bloemfontein for a few weeks. He also wanted to repair the railway links to the Cape before he proceeded further north.

THE CAPE FRONT

The evacuation of the Cape Colony

After the heavy fighting at Stormberg there were only minor clashes of little importance on the Cape front. The British forces here were prepared to wait to receive news of developments on the other fronts before launching a new attack. The offensive initiated by Roberts gave these forces the opportunity they had been waiting for.

On his march to Bloemfontein Roberts threatened to move behind the commandos that were based at Colesberg and Stormberg. They did not realise that if they had just moved faster than the British forces they could very easily have invaded deeper into the Cape Colony.

Instead of doing this, the commandos began to retreat into the Free State. On 28 February the British were able to

A British armoured train

occupy Colesberg and by 5 March they entered Stormberg. The retreat of the republican forces was a great help to Roberts because shortly after taking Bloemfontein, the railway communication between the town and the Cape harbours could be restored. The transportation of their military supplies was obviously of vital importance to the British forces in Bloemfontein.

THE NATAL FRONT

The relief of Ladysmith

After his defeat at Vaalkrans it finally got through to Buller that the best way to relieve Ladysmith was to drive back the left wing of the republican force which was drawn up to the south of the Tugela River on Hlangwane and other nearby ridges. If he could succeed in doing this he would be able to use his artillery to bombard their positions on the north of the river and so destroy the republican front.

Buller's fourth attempt to relieve Ladysmith began on 17 February with an attack on the republican entrenchments to the east of Hlangwane. Although the commandos put up a spirited defence, they eventually had to succumb to the stronger force, evacuate their positions and fall back across the Tugela. In this way Hlangwane also fell to the British on 18 February. For Botha, who again commanded the defence against the British attack, the loss of this particular entrenchment was a cruel blow.

His position was to become even more difficult in the next few days because, when Roberts broke through in the Free State, a large number of burghers had to be withdrawn from the Natal front to go to the western front. While Buller's position was getting stronger as more troops arrived, Botha's force was weakened by the transfer of these commandos. Botha nevertheless decided to make the enemy pay dearly for every step of progress they made. His left wing was now deployed on Pietershoogte, east of Colenso. Buller meanwhile dispatched a strong force over the Tugela and on 23 February he once again went on the attack. Despite their numerical disadvantage the Boers, as of old, stood firm and gave the enemy a reception for which they were certainly not prepared. The Krugersdorp commando in particular acquitted itself with great distinction. The British suffered heavy losses and were simply unable to make any progress. If Botha had had more burghers at his disposal, he could easily have managed to drive the British back over the Tugela River. The British, of course, could still bring in more reinforcements, while the burghers were exhausted because of the continual fighting. This meant that the fortunes of war turned even further against the Boers. Buller simply had to keep on attacking, regardless of his losses, and he would eventually break the enemy's resistance. And this is exactly what happened. The republican forces finally had to give way and on 1 March, Ladysmith was relieved. For both Buller and White it was a triumphant day.

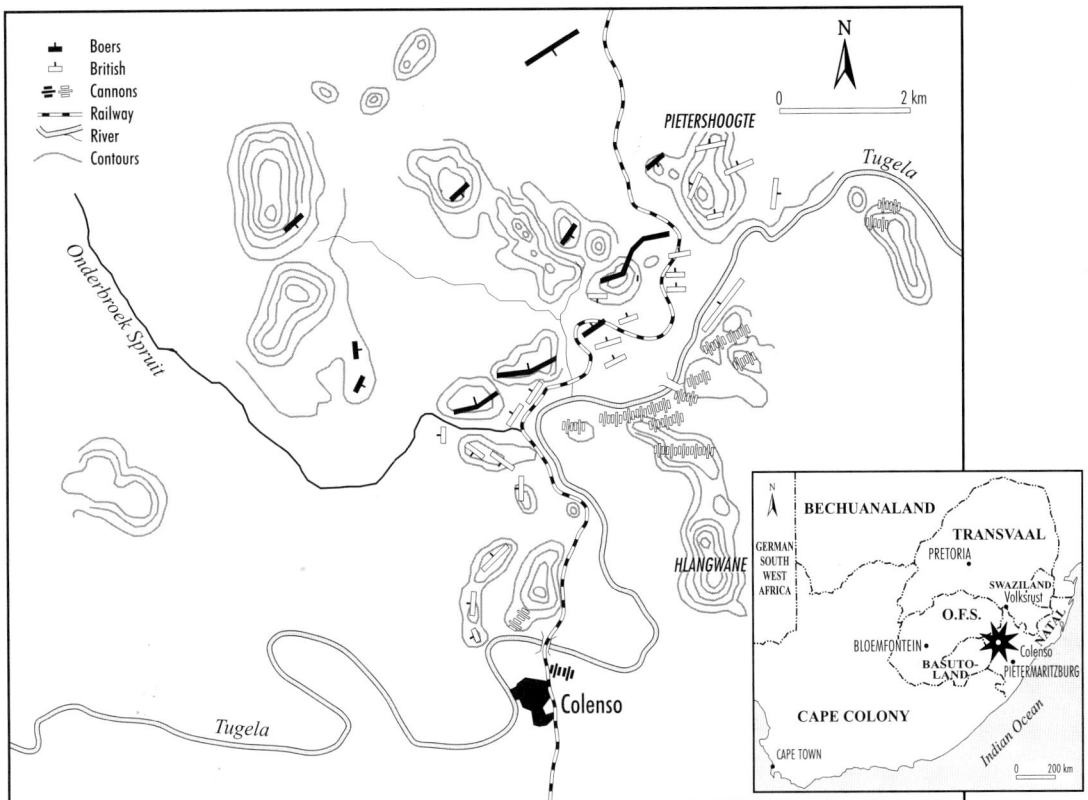

Pietershoogte, February 1900

Botha's commandos had to fall back quickly. The Free Staters dispersed in the direction of the Drakensberg Mountains, while the Transvalers took up new entrenchments in the Biggarsberg Mountains. With the occupation of Bloemfontein and the relief of Ladysmith the first phase of the British offensive was over. After so many weeks of exertion the troops under Roberts and Buller needed to rest and a few weeks of comparative quiet settled over the theatre of war.

CHAPTER V
FROM BLOEMFONTEIN TO PRETORIA

DE WET ON THE ATTACK

The new strategy

The British troops in the Free State and the Transvaal were forced to take a rest and this gave De Wet, who had continued the struggle tirelessly, an opportunity which he used to the full. As leader of the Free State commandos, he now began to implement a new method of warfare which should have been followed right from the beginning of the war.

De Wet's strategy can be summarised briefly. Firstly, the war would in the future be fought with mobile mounted commandos which could cover great distances in a day. Secondly, unlike the methods used in the early part of the war, defensive tactics would be used as seldom as possible. De Wet would attack whenever he could. Thirdly, De Wet decided that because he and his mounted commandos were so much more mobile than the British, great advantage could be gained by moving in behind the enemy and attacking from the rear. Gone was the time when the commandos had to move slowly because the burghers had brought their wagons along with them. From now on De Wet's commandos would move so quickly that the enemy would never really know where to look for them.

Sannaspos

Once he had given his burghers a short rest, De Wet was ready to go out on the attack. After the occupation of Bloemfontein Roberts had sent a division of troops under General Broadwood in the direction of Thaba Nchu and Ladybrand. However, because this column was in danger of being cut off, Broadwood had decided to return to Bloemfontein. His progress was hampered by the many wagons and carts that he had with him. De Wet decided to teach Broadwood a lesson.

For the encounter De Wet chose a site called Sannaspos, which was just less than 32 kilometers east of Bloemfontein. Early in the morning of 31 March De Wet and about 400 men took up their positions in the almost-dry bed of the Koringspruit. Here De Wet was completely hidden from the enemy and he was directly between Broadwood and his destination, Bloemfontein. The remaining 1200 of De Wet's burghers would bombard Broadwood with cannon fire to drive them in the direction of Koringspruit where they would then be finished off.

De Wet's plan was a brilliant success. As soon as the first bombs landed in his camp Broadwood hastily set off for Bloemfontein into the waiting arms of De Wet. When the first cart tried to cross the Koringspruit an armed burgher suddenly appeared, sat next to the driver and ordered him to drive in a certain direction. This was done with all the wagons and carts. After a while 200 foot soldiers arrived and were promptly captured and disarmed before they realised exactly what was happening. The crew of a battery of five cannons was also captured and these cannons were very useful booty indeed.

While all this was going on in the Koringspruit drift, the other columns became suspicious that something was amiss, and the burghers then began their fire. The British were taken completely by surprise and suffered heavy losses. Meanwhile the rest of De Wet's force also appeared on the scene and attacked Broadwood. There was now only one option open to him: he had to try to reach Bloemfontein at all costs. Because there were too few burghers in the Koringspruit to form a long enough line, the British were able to rush to another drift and managed to escape.

Sannaspos, 31 March 1900

63

It was a heavy defeat and Broadwood lost a third of his force of 1 800 men.

Reddersburg

De Wet's brillant victory at Sannaspos gave the burghers new hope and many of those who had gone home after the fall of Bloemfontein returned to take up arms again.

De Wet was determined to deal the enemy many more such blows. His next victim was Captain McWhinnie who had occupied Dewetsdorp with a force of more than 400 men. When the captain heard of the disaster that had befallen Broadwood at Sannaspos, he thought it would perhaps be wise to leave Dewetsdorp and fall back to join the troops that had regrouped along the railway line between the Orange River and Bloem-fontein.

It was then that De Wet proved conclusively that he could move far more quickly than his opponents. In the vicinity of Reddersburg on 4 April he caught up with McWhinnie's force, surrounded it and after a sharp struggle forced it to surrender. Again it was an efficient piece of work, particularly considering that it took place perilously close to a strong enemy force under Gatacre. Because Roberts felt that Gatacre had not reacted energetically enough, Gatacre was later relieved of his command and sent back to Britain.

Wepener

With this second success De Wet had now cleared practically all the British troops from the entire southern Free State between the railway line and the border of Basutoland (now Lesotho). He wanted to use this opportunity to cross the Orange River and advance into the Cape Colony.

This would make Roberts's position in Bloemfontein very difficult because De Wet would then be able to cut off his railway communication. But Steyn was afraid that the Transvalers would complain that they had been left to defend the Free State alone.

Therefore De Wet was unable to carry out this excellent plan and instead he had to take another line of action which, as he himself admitted in his book on the war, proved to be unwise. On 9 April he decided to besiege the British force that was still in Wepener and try to force them to surrender.

The garrison under Colonel Dalgety was besieged for sixteen days, but once again the Boers showed that they could not maintain strict discipline. When a British force arrived on 25 April to relieve the garrison, the commandos had to flee.

LORD ROBERTS TAKES THE OFFENSIVE AGAIN

The second phase

While De Wet was stirring up trouble for the British in the southern Free State, Roberts continued undaunted with his preparations for the second phase of the offensive which would take him through to Pretoria. And Roberts was confident that once he had the Transvaal capital in his possession, it would mean the end of the war because the republican forces would certainly surrender.

The second phase of the British offensive took the form of a massive march along both sides of the railway line that runs from Bloemfontein to the north. The left wing of Roberts's army was to be protected by Methuen who would move along south of the Vaal River via Boshof, Hoopstad and Bothaville. North of the Vaal River General Hunter would invade the Transvaal with a large force and travel via Christiana and Bloemhof to Klerksdorp and Potchefstroom. Once Roberts's troops had made some progress, another force under General Rundle would advance into the eastern Free State. At the same time Buller would begin with a new offensive in Natal and would later join Roberts's forces in the Transvaal.

Roberts made sure that he had a vastly superior force at his disposal before he began his second offensive. The columns under his command as well as those under Methuen and Hunter numbered about 100 000 men. In Natal Buller had a force of about 50 000.

Against this massive force, the republican commanders could apparently only muster about 30 000 men. Botha, who had been appointed to the

65

rank of commandant-general in charge of the Transvaal commandos when Joubert died on 27 March, now left the Natal front and went to the Free State. He and De Wet were to work together for a brief period.

Vet River and Sand River

On 3 May the huge force that Roberts planned to take up to Pretoria finally got under way. The Free State plains did not really provide many places where the commandos could use the terrain to try to harass the enemy. In fact the rivers which criss-crossed the plains were the only natural obstacles in the path of the British forces. The first river that had to be forded was the Vet River. There were only a few commandos positioned there in the hope that they would be able to impede the march. The result was that the British troops had little trouble crossing the river on 5 May.

Botha and De Wet decided to draw up their forces on the northern bank of the Sand River and come to blows there with Roberts. It was to be Botha's first exchange outside Natal where he had been in opposition to the tardy Buller. Botha thus had no experience of Roberts's new tactics of skirting around the Boer entrenchments with his cavalry. The positions that the Boers took up along the Sand River were reasonably secure, but Roberts had no intention of being cornered there. He had noticed that Botha's right wing did not stretch very far to the west. Against Buller this would have been of little consequence, but against Roberts it was fatal.

On 10 May the British launched their attack. French crossed the Sand River to the west of the right wing of the republican forces with a strong cavalry division and immediately advanced towards Kroonstad, travelling over the Free State plains where the goldfields now lie. As a result the commandos had to abandon their positions hastily to escape the threatened encirclement. By 12 May the British were able to occupy Kroonstad, and Steyn and the Free State government took refuge in Heilbron. It was then agreed that the Transvaal commandos under Botha would retreat from the British and move to the north, while the Free Staters would go east. De Wet was now determined to get behind Roberts.

Johannesburg

Roberts delayed for only a little over a week in Kroonstad before he resumed the march to Pretoria. He encountered little resistance and by 27 May his advance guard was able to cross the Vaal River at Vereeniging. Botha decided to make another attempt to halt the British forces in the ridges south of Johannesburg. On 29 May a hard battle raged all day long on the broad front stretching from south of Krugersdorp to Germiston, but when for the umpteenth time the British began their encircling manoeuvres, the commandos had to abandon their positions. On 31 May Roberts entered Johannesburg.

Pretoria

The City of Gold was not Roberts's final objective. He wanted to reach Pretoria because he thought that when he occupied the Transvaal capital the republican forces would give up and submit to his control. So he pushed through to Pretoria. Botha decided not to defend the town and retreated with the majority of his men along the Delagoa Bay railway line. The ageing Kruger was now also compelled to leave Pretoria and he went to Machadodorp with the other members of his government where he was to live for a number of months in a railway coach.

The British troops occupy Pretoria

On 5 June the forces under Roberts were thus able to march into Pretoria unchallenged. According to the British predictions this should have been the end of the war. But no request for submission was forthcoming from the republican governments and the war had to continue. This marked the beginning of the third phase of the British offensive.

CHAPTER VI
THE WAR CONTINUES

With the occupation of Pretoria Roberts gained possession of a sizeable portion of the two republics. In the Free State it was only the eastern districts such as Senekal, Ficksburg, Bethlehem, Frankfort, Vrede and Harrismith that were not in British hands. In the Transvaal nearly all the western and southern districts had been occupied and Mafeking was relieved on 17 May after a heroic defence. The rest of the Transvaal was still free of enemy control, but it was questionable just how long this could last because in early June Buller left Natal and began to move closer to the Transvaal border, making preparations to occupy the south-eastern districts.

Despite Britain's strong position, it became clear to Roberts soon after the fall of Pretoria that the war was not yet over, as he had thought it would be. He was therefore obliged to occupy those parts of the two republics that were still free, in the hope that this would stop the Boer resistance. The British offensive thus moved into its third phase.

THE FREE STATE

The Boers on the attack once again

In May, when Roberts started his rapid advance to Pretoria, he assigned the task of capturing the eastern Free State districts to Rundle. Rundle first went from Thaba Nchu to Ficksburg and once he had taken the town he moved northwards to Senekal, which he occupied on 25 May.

Thus far he had met with practically no resistance, but on 29 May just outside Senekal he suddenly ran into a commando under General A.J. de Villiers. De Villiers, who was an exceptionally brave man, gave his opponent a severe drubbing and after suffering heavy losses, Rundle was forced to flee. As far as the British were concerned this was proof that the struggle in the Free State was far from over.

Two days later on 31 May, another unpleasant surprise awaited the British. On their northward march they had also left behind a garrison, the Imperial Yeomanry Regiment, at Lindley. General Piet de Wet's eye now fell on this 500-strong force. He quickly mustered a few commandos and surrounded the garrison. The Imperial Yeomanry finally surrendered after being mercilessly bombarded for three days. This success also gave the burghers new courage.

Rooiwal

The most active of the Free State commanders was still C.R. de Wet. When Roberts crossed the Vaal River at the end of May, De Wet had the chance he had been waiting for. He could now take action behind Roberts's back and do as much damage as he possibly could.

General Christiaan de Wet

The British forces in Johannesburg and Pretoria were now dependant on the railway which ran from the Cape harbours via Bloemfontein and Kroonstad to the north, for the transportation of all their military supplies. Because the republican forces had destroyed a number of bridges as they retreated, the supplies destined for Johannesburg and Pretoria were delayed and there was a big stockpile of goods at Rooiwal station on the southern side of the Vaal River. This did not escape De Wet's eagle eye and he decided to go and claim all the wonderful goods that were meant for Roberts and his soldiers.

On his way to the station on 4 June, De Wet succeeded in forcing a convoy heading towards Heilbron to surrender without even firing a single shot. But De Wet was aiming for bigger booty and he made careful preparations for the attack on Rooiwal station.

It was planned that on 7 June two of his subordinates would attack the small British forces that were camped a few kilometers away on either side of the river and force them to surrender. This was successfully accomplished. De Wet then led the attack on Rooiwal station himself and the division that was guarding the goods eventually had to surrender after a fight lasting a few hours. Goods of considerable value were now in De Wet's hands and long afterwards he even used some of the ammunition which he had found at Rooiwal and hidden nearby against the British.

For Roberts and his troops the sacrifice of their military supplies was a bitter lesson that in future they would have to reckon with De Wet in every situation.

Bethlehem and General Prinsloo's surrender

Because he was being harassed from behind by the commandos, Roberts decided that the remaining parts of the Free State should also be occupied. This, in his view, would stop the resistance. Strong British forces were thus deployed to effect the occupation of the eastern Free State.

The town of Bethlehem was the main target of the British. De Wet had also gathered a number of commandos there and on 6 July heavy fighting broke out.

The fighting continued until the next day, but eventually the burghers had to give way to the superior force. The British troops which came from the north-east, the north and the north-west then forced the commandos back into the mountains near Fouriesburg. There they were in an extremely perilous position, because they were in danger of being completely surrounded by the British. But De Wet certainly did not plan to be caught and took timeous steps to make sure that he and Steyn, who by now regularly accompanied the commandos in the field, and a few thousand burghers were able to slip adroitly through the enemy lines to get behind them again.

The order from De Wet was that the other commandos should follow his example, which could have easily been done if their commanders had been men of courage. A council of war made up of officers nevertheless decided to choose General Marthinus Prinsloo as their commander.

A weaker choice could hardly have been made because Prinsloo certainly had no talent at all in this direction. The action he took was woeful and he did not make the slightest attempt to break through the British lines. About 1 500 men who realised what would happen under a man like Prinsloo managed to escape without much difficulty.
Prinsloo then conducted negotiations with the British commander and on 30 July he and his 4 000 men surrendered.

After the surrender at Paardeberg, this capitulation in the mountains at Fouriesburg was the heaviest blow that hit the republican forces in 1900. The capture of such a large number of men by the British had an extremely demoralising effect on the burghers who were still in the field.

With Prinsloo's surrender all the towns in the eastern part of the Free State fell into British hands.

The first De Wet hunt

De Wet's actions had caused the British so much trouble that they decided to put him out of action for good. They realised that if they could catch him, the resistance in the Free State would probably disintegrate. Immediately after he had slipped through the British net, Roberts ordered that a large number of columns go out to capture De Wet.

British forces came in from every side in an attempt to surround and capture the Boer general and the hunt soon stretched right across the Free State. Like a speedy flyhalf who runs right through the opponent's team without having a finger laid on him, De Wet evaded one British force after the other. He moved around so quickly and so deceptive was he in his movements, that no single British column could ever succeed in keeping contact with him for more than 24 hours.

This son of the veld, who knew well nigh every stone in the Free State, never succumbed to fatigue. To sleep for a few minutes on his horse's back was enough for him. When he was on the move he sent out his commando scouts far and wide to keep him in touch with the movements of the enemy. At every moment of the day or night he knew precisely where the British forces were and what they planned to do. While he knew everything about the British forces, they were seldom able to find out where he was at any given moment. And when an opportunity arose he could invariably trap a British column in an untoward manner and deal it a heavy blow.

General de Wet's commando crosses the Orange Rivier

With bated breath millions of people outside South Africa followed accounts of how one British commander after the other suffered at the hands of a man who, although he had no military training, nevertheless outclassed all the commanders that the British sent against him.

This was also the case on the following occasion. De Wet was pursued by the British forces in the Free State and was driven over the Vaal River.

71

There new enemy forces which came from Potchefstroom and the Witwatersrand continued the chase. But De Wet outwitted them and crossed the Magaliesberg Mountains. Here he was able to enjoy safety and rest for a short while.

At this stage Steyn, who had accompanied De Wet for the entire expedition, took his leave because he wanted to visit Kruger who was still in Machadodorp. De Wet planned to return to the Free State, and soon he was being followed again by the British forces. There was only one way to give them the slip: he had to cross the high Magaliesberg Mountains. De Wet asked an old black man: "Can we get over them?" The reply was that only the baboons could do so. "If a baboon can cross, then so can we," said De Wet to his burghers. And indeed they did. By 21 August, De Wet was crossing the Vaal River again.

EASTERN TRANSVAAL

Diamond Hill (Donkerhoek)

When there was no surrender of the Boer commandos following the occupation of Pretoria, Roberts was forced to continue the struggle by conquering the remainder of the Transvaal. To the east, north and west of Pretoria there were still commandos that had to be dealt with.

Botha himself was at the head of the commandos that were active along the railway to Delagoa Bay. The burghers had taken up strong positions there on a series of ridges and were waiting for the British attack.

Botha still believed in the use of trench warfare to stop the enemy advance, so there was a marked difference between his tactics and those of De Wet.

But the lesson that he had learned at Sand River was enough to teach Botha to be careful not to let the British forces skirt around the wings of his army so easily. This was in fact exactly what Roberts was planning to do for the umpteenth time.

On 11 June the battle known as Donkerhoek or Diamond Hill began. The British forces tried to go around both wings of the opposition, but Botha out in a long line so that the British could not apply their usual tactics.

When the sun eventually went down, Roberts was still as far from victory as he had been that morning. The fight continued the next day and again Botha refused to budge. However, the superior British force slowly turned the tide in favour of Roberts and on the night of 12 June the Boers evacuated their positions and fell back further to the east.

Dalmanutha

Because the British had had so much trouble from De Wet, Roberts decided to try to get rid of him and sent a strong force into the Free State. In the event, they were unable to catch him, as has been shown already. The net result was that for the time being Roberts did not move further along the railway to Delagoa Bay, and Botha was left in peace.

While Roberts was obliged to remain inactive, Buller crossed the border and moved further into the Transvaal. With one portion of his army he advanced in the direction of Standerton and Heidelberg in order to join Roberts's troops. With the other he moved north-east towards the Delagoa Bay line. He could therefore easily get behind Botha, who was delaying in the region of Balmoral after the battle of Diamond Hill.

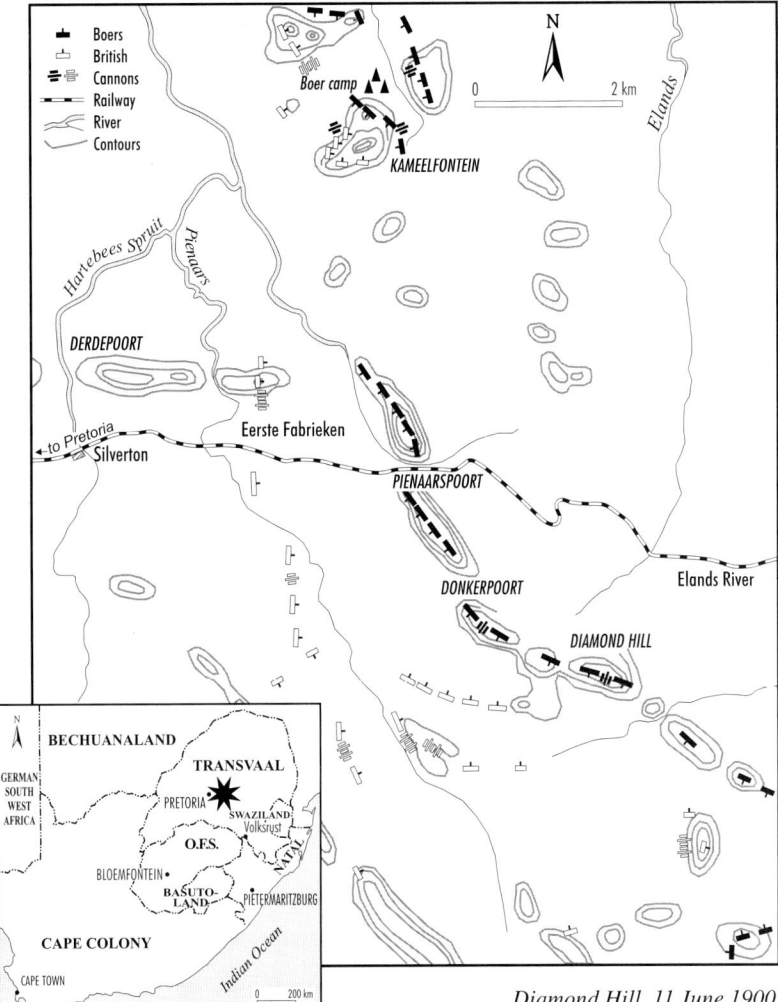

Diamond Hill, 11 June 1900

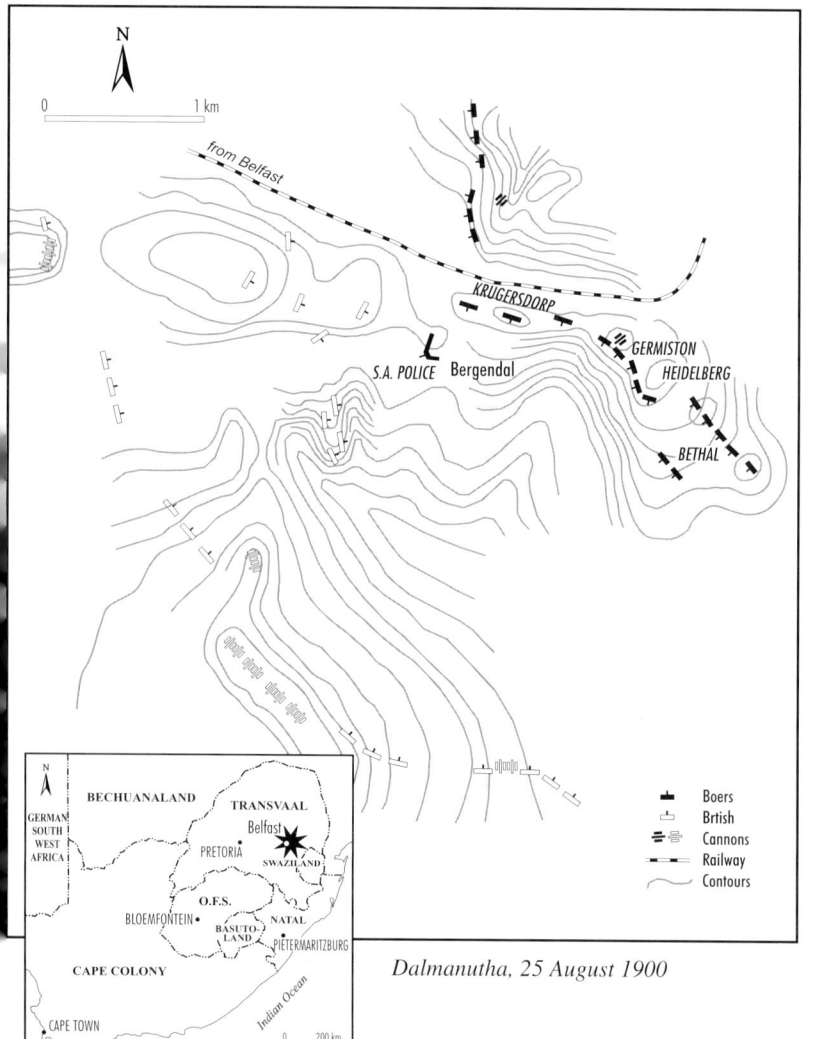

Dalmanutha, 25 August 1900

Botha felt that under the circumstances it was wise to fall back slowly along the railway line, and on 27 July the British forces moved unhindered into Middelburg. But the hunt for De Wet was still Roberts's first priority so he decided not to go any further.

It was only in the second half of August that the British again focused their attention on Botha's men. A decision was taken to join the forces which came from the direction of Middelburg (Transvaal) under Roberts, and those from the Ermelo side under Buller. Botha decided to take on the enemy near Belfast in the battle known as Dalmanutha.

The battle began on 21 August and although the British as usual outnumbered the Boers by far, they initially made no progress. Once again Botha showed that he was equal to the task when pitted against the best of the British generals. Roberts could only rescue the situation by making use of his superior artillery. The key to the republican positions was a small hill which was occupied by 74 members of the Johannesburg Police under the orders of Commandant Philip Oosthuizen and Lieutenant F. Pohlman. On the morning of 27 August the hill was bombarded worse than ever before by the cannons. After a few hours the infantry went on the attack thinking that they would easily wipe out the handful of men. But their hopes were soon dashed because they were met with such heavy gunfire that caused such grave losses that reinforcements had to be brought in. Johannesburg's constables kept firing until they were overwhelmed. Most of them died a heroic death.

After the conquest of his entrenchments, Botha retreated in the direction of Lydenburg. This was to be the last conventional battle in which he was involved. On 24 September the British columns reached Komatipoort on the Mozambique border and thereby completed the conquest of the entire Transvaal to the south of the railway.

WESTERN TRANSVAAL

In the previous chapter it was mentioned that when Roberts advanced from Bloemfontein to Pretoria, Hunter simultaneously moved with a strong force into the western districts of the Transvaal. Yet another British division under Colonel B.T. Mahon set off from Fourteen Streams to relieve Mafeking. When this had been successfully accomplished on 17 May, other British troops also advanced against the Transvaal from this side. The result of these attacks was that all the important western Transvaal towns such as Klerksdorp, Potchefstroom, Lichtenburg and Rustenburg were in British hands before the end of June.

At the outset no major battles took place in this part of the Transvaal. After the battle of Donkerpoort De la Rey returned to these districts and reorganised the commandos there. From then on he took the leadership of the region on his shoulders. His arrival made a big difference to the situation because De la Rey had already proved himself as one of the most able republican commanders. Within a few months De la Rey was again ready to take full control in major battles.

CHAPTER VII
THE GUERRILLA WAR BEGINS

NEW CIRCUMSTANCES

The situation in September 1900

By September 1900 the British forces were already in possession of both republics with the exception of the northern districts of the Transvaal. But the circumstances of this occupation were curious. The British did not really possess anything more than the ground on which their columns stood at any particular moment. As soon as a column left a particular district, the British authority there also disappeared. The area of the republics was so large that the British needed far more than 250 000 men to keep full control of every kilometre. It was impossible for them to form close-knit lines stretching unbroken over these vast distances. This gave the commandos the opportunity to slip through widely spaced columns and burghers could return to regions that had previously been occupied by the British. It was therefore a continuation of the strategy that De Wet had initiated early in 1900 — to move more quickly than the enemy and attack them from the rear.

The British expectation that the war would come to an end once they had occupied the major part of the republics did not materialise. On the other hand the republican commanders soon realised the implications of this: opportunities were there for the taking because the British could not feasibly occupy every part of the Free State and Transvaal all the time. The commandos were told to return to their home regions throughout the two republics and when a suitable opportunity arose they should be ready to take up the struggle against the enemy.

De Wet came to this decision in September, immediately after returning to the Free State from the Transvaal. He first made extensive changes to the republican military system. Formerly, the burghers had chosen their own officers. This did not work well in practice because men who were ill equipped were often selected. De Wet himself now took over the appointment of officers and made it clear that he would only choose men who had shown that they had the necessary ability. Under him he also named three assistant chief-commandants who had to go to the southern and western parts of the Free State to reconstitute commandos among those burghers who had laid down their arms and gone back to their farms. The three officers named were General Piet Fourie, Judge J.B.M. Hertzog and Field-Cornet C.C.J. Badenhorst, and they did indeed succeed in setting up new commandos.

After the battle of Dalmanutha Botha also came to the realisation that the war would now have to be conducted differently. He decided that guerrilla warfare would be the best way to take on the enemy and he too disbanded his force and sent the commandos back to their own districts with orders to tackle the enemy there. In the Transvaal it was also decided that Botha should be responsible for the appointment of officers. He took the opportunity to get rid of a number of incompetent officers and replace them with men who had already shown that they possessed the necessary military talent. De la Rey, with the rank of assistant commandant-general, was to be responsible for the action in the western part of the Transvaal, while assistant commandant-general C.F. Beyers would take responsibility for the northern Transvaal.

From September 1900 onwards the war thus took on a completely different character compared with the situation thus far. The closed line, for example, was no longer used and the troops of the two opposing parties moved around far more. It was now the strategy of the republican commandos to do as much damage to the enemy as possible. When the British advanced with their vastly superior numbers, the commandos simply gave way and promptly made themselves very difficult to find. If a British column became isolated in any way, the commandos surrounded it like a swarm of bees and usually dealt it a merciless blow — then the commandos would disappear again before help could arrive for the startled column. A British column could seldom march out without its route being kept under constant surveillance from afar by Boer scouts who would then report to their officers on every move the enemy made. This strategy, known as guerrilla warfare, would be followed by the republican forces right until the end of the war.

President Kruger and President Steyn

The decision to wage a guerrilla war placed the Transvaal government in a difficult position. The aged Kruger did not have the physical strength to move around with the commandos. The question therefore was how best to prevent his falling into the hands of the British. The Executive Council decided in September that Kruger should go to Delagoa Bay and from there sail to Europe, where he would be able to plead the republican cause with the various governments. He should try to persuade them to act as arbiters in restoring peace in South Africa with the maintenance of republican independence.

Steyn, who as has been mentioned had left De Wet north of the Magaliesberg, also impressed upon Kruger that he should go to Europe. Kruger finally agreed and left for Delagoa Bay. His activities in Europe will be discussed in the last chapter.

Kruger's departure meant that Steyn came even more prominently to the fore than he had at the beginning of the war. In fact he personified the Afrikaners' freedom struggle. After Heilbron had also fallen to the British, Steyn and his government joined the commandos and endured all the hardships and suffering together with the burghers. Steyn was prepared to make the supreme sacrifice to retain the independence of the republics. As far as he was concerned there was no question about it: the struggle simply had to go on until the British were prepared to conclude a peace with the recognition of the independence of the two republics. His leadership in the struggle was an inspiration to everyone. He was never downhearted and he believed steadfastly that the republican ideal would eventually be realised. His role in the war elevated him to one of the greatest Afrikaner heroes.

Lord Roberts

Lord Roberts and Lord Kitchener

Kruger was not the only leader to leave the South African coast in the last months of 1900. He was soon to be followed by Roberts. Once his forces had conquered the major portion of both republics, Roberts decided that the war was over and all that remained to do was a little clearing up. He decided to leave that to Kitchener, and in November he relinquished his command.

Seldom has a military commander made such an error of judgement. Just as the republican forces were set to move into a new phase of their resistance by using guerrilla warfare, Roberts decided that everything was under control and he could return to Britain. Little did he know at the time that the war would still continue for nearly a year and a half.

For the remainder of the war the British forces in South Africa were under the command of Kitchener.

IN THE FREE STATE

De Wet suffers some setbacks

The guerrilla war did not begin too well for De Wet. After spending most of September reorganising the Free State forces, he began a new initiative. Most of his activities were in the northern districts where he was also in close communication with the commandos that were fighting in the western Transvaal. In mid-October he and General Piet Liebenberg decided to join up to attack a British force under Barton which was stationed at Frederikstad on the railway line near Potchefstroom. The British were well positioned and unbeknown to the Boers they were prepared for an attack. The republican forces surrounded Barton and his men for five days — from 21 to 26 October — and then the combined attack failed because of poor cooperation among the Boers. With that, a new force also arrived to relieve Barton and De Wet was forced to retreat rapidly into Free State territory. He did not suffer this setback with good grace.

After his meeting with Kruger in the eastern Transvaal Steyn now returned and joined De Wet. At this stage De Wet received a report that Fourie and Hertzog had again drawn up their commandos in the southern parts of the Free State. This influenced his decision to implement a plan he had cherished for a long time: to invade the Cape Colony.

Before he could go ahead with this, De Wet suffered a second setback. He and Steyn were with a commando of 800 men south of the Vals River near Bothaville when they went to sleep on the night of 5 November. A British force of about 1 200 men under Colonel Le Gallais had encamped on the northern side of the river. De Wet placed a number of sentries between the two camps so that he could be warned if the enemy should stir. But the British were one step ahead of the Boers.

By daybreak on the morning of 6 November the Boer sentries returned with the news that all was still quiet. De Wet had no sooner received the report than his burghers, many of whom were still fast asleep, were attacked by vicious enemy fire. The result was such a state of panic among the burghers that all De Wet's attempts to calm the men and get them to attack the enemy were doomed to failure. They simply fled, leaving everything behind, including five cannons. Many men were unable to escape and were captured by the British.

The British were delighted that at last they had succeeded in dealing a blow to the elusive De Wet, but Le Gallais, who had achieved the victory, died in the encounter.

The first attempt to invade the Cape Colony

De Wet did not let his defeat at Bothaville deter him and immediately set about getting everything ready for his plan to invade the Cape Colony. With his invasion he wanted to shift the theatre of war from the republics back into British territory because he realised that this would force the British military leaders to withdraw troops from the Transvaal and Free State in order to send them to the Cape. Furthermore, when the commandos arrived on the southern side of the Orange River there were bound to be many Cape Afrikaners who would take up arms to help their fellow Afrikaners. These factors could work in the Boers' favour.

On 13 November De Wet met the commandos at Doringberg near Ventersburg. With about 1 500 men he then set off to the south. His first goal was Dewetsdorp and there on 29 November he surrounded a garrison of almost 500 men and finally forced them to surrender after a battle lasting until 22 November. The two cannons and large quantities of ammunition that he took were particularly valuable booty.

De Wet then moved further south as quickly as his horses could gallop. The British military leaders realised what was happening and immediately dispatched a strong force under General C.E. Knox by train to the south in an effort to prevent an invasion of the Cape Colony. One can clearly see how uneven the struggle was at the time: the British had all the advantages on their side.

The British could make use of trains; De Wet had to rely on his horses. But despite this the British were unable to catch him.

Hertzog now joined De Wet with a small commando and they arranged that they would try to cross the Orange River separately and move into the Cape. Hertzog succeeded: he managed to cross the river quickly and moved into British territory. Time and again he managed to shake off the British columns that pursued him and he eventually reached the Atlantic Ocean at Lamberts Bay. Here he turned back to the north again.

De Wet had less success. Heavy rains began to fall and although this also hampered the British pursuit, to his great disappointment De Wet had to admit that the natural elements had foiled his plans

General De Wet's first invasion of the Cape Colony

to get into the Cape. As a result of the heavy rain the Orange River was in flood and it would have been absolutely impossible for the horsemen to cross. To make matters even worse the British were already deployed on the southern side of the river, waiting at the ready to prevent any possible attempt the commandos might make to ford the river. And the force under Knox was also fast approaching from the rear. The plan to invade the Cape Colony had of necessity to be abandoned. Now the major concern was not to be caught by the advancing British forces. De Wet's position was critical because he was trapped in the triangle formed by the confluence of the Orange River, the Caledon River and the border of Basutoland (now Lesotho). But De Wet instinctively knew how to escape such a situation. No enemy columns could move as swiftly as he could and, with a few long expeditions that placed very high demands on both the men and their animals, he succeeded in leaving his pursuers far behind and moved north once more.

Although De Wet had failed in his bid to invade the Cape, he managed to get a number of burghers who lived beyond the Orange River to join up.

81

Because the British were concentrating all their attention on De Wet, a small commando under General P.H. Kritzinger and Commandant Gideon Scheepers was able to remain behind unnoticed.

Once the majority of the British troops had moved north in pursuit of De Wet, and when the level of the Orange River had returned to normal again, these two men and their burghers could move into the Cape Colony.

De Wet now moved quickly northwards, but his problems were not yet over. To shake off the enemy completely he first had to devise a way to get through the front line which the British had laid between Bloemfontein and Thaba Nchu. De Wet decided to stage his breakthrough at Springkaansnek in the early hours of the morning of 14 December. The burghers would have to rush between two forts over a distance of about three kilometres while the British soldiers fired a hail of bullets at them.

Amazingly, only one man was wounded and De Wet achieved his objective, passing through safely.

The second attempt to invade the Cape Colony

It was certainly a very keen disappointment for De Wet that his first attempt to invade the Cape had ended in failure. But he refused to abandon the idea and decided that early in 1901 he would make another attempt.

It had become necessary to provide some relief for the two republics because, as will be shown in the next chapter, Kitchener had decided upon a new strategy to counter the Boers' guerrilla warfare.

On 25 January 1901 a number of Free State commandos under De Wet were drawn up at Doringberg waiting to begin the journey southwards for the second time. When Kitchener realised that De Wet had the Cape in his sights once more, he not only sent in a strong body of troops to follow the commandos but also time and again put new forces between De Wet and his objective. The British forces could of course be transported by train while the burghers only had their horses.

Time and time again De Wet, with his greater mobility, outwitted Knox, who had once more been charged with taking action against him. De Wet easily broke through the forts between Thaba Nchu and Bloemfontein and then moved to the south as quickly as possible. Thereafter he could not be stopped. Kitchener tried sending in troops from all sides — even from the Transvaal — to the Orange River area to try to prevent the Boer progress. Even before De Wet started approaching, the British had formed a long line by occupying nearly all the routes he might conceivably have used. But De Wet was kept very well informed of all these by his scouts. It was in circumstances such as this that he was at his most resourceful. He had the enemy utterly confused by pretending first that he was about to go in a southerly direction and then quickly moving off to the west. On 10 February he crossed the Orange River near Petrusville.

De Wet had, to a limited extent, realised his great ideal. Now the big question was just how far he and his men would be able to penetrate into the Cape Colony.

General De Wet's second invasion of the Cape Colony

When the British commanders realised that they had been outwitted by De Wet they immediately sent their troops by train to the area between De Aar and Orange River station hoping to prevent him from crossing the railway line. Again they were misled. On the night of 14 February De Wet and his commando crossed the line safely.

Once more it was the weather that helped the British. The rain came down in torrents and impeded the progress of the commando, but even, worse, it made every little rivulet into a surging stream. When De Wet crossed the railway he continued in a westerly direction to try to elude the British columns. This meant that he now found himself faced by the wide bend of the Orange River just before its confluence with the Vaal. To avoid being checked by the Orange River again, De Wet was forced to move south, thus penetrating deeper into the Cape, but here he was blocked by a tributary of the Orange, the Brak River, and there was not the slightest possiblity of crossing. And from the rear the British columns were rapidly

83

getting nearer. Faced by the Brak River in full flood, De Wet was desperate: seldom before had he been in such a critical situation. But for the umpteenth time he found a way out: he went quickly in the direction of the Orange River and then moved upstream. However, the circumstances forced him to abandon his plans to invade the Cape Colony.

For now the first and most important goal was to escape the attentions of the British force behind him and to get back into the Free State again. This was certainly one of the most demanding tasks De Wet had faced, because his men and animals had already been on trek practically day and night for the best part of a month and some of the burghers were so exhausted and discouraged that it was only with the greatest effort of will that they were able to continue. By moving upstream along the Orange River, De Wet again had to cross the railway line between Kimberley and De Aar. A long night march saw the commando safely over and out of reach of the pursuing British who could not understand how the Boers had managed to evade their attempted encirclement.

De Wet now only had to find a drift so that he could get back into the Free State. At this stage he was rejoined by Hertzog. When the British discovered that De Wet had eluded them yet again they sent their forces by train to Colesberg and other places in a new attempt to trap the Boers against the Orange River. But on 28 February, before the British troops could be properly deployed, the Boer commander succeeded in crossing the river with his entire commando, and he moved into the Free State. The British troops were then promptly sent off by train again — this time to Springfontein with orders to cut off the commando's journey to the north.

But this effort was in vain. Long before the British could get anywhere near De Wet he was already north of Bloemfontein and beyond the reach of the enemy.

De Wet's second attempt to invade the Cape Colony was an epic journey that can be regarded as his greatest achievement. To be followed for a month by an enemy which possessed a vastly superior force, could make use of the trains and was assisted by the elements, was a test which only a commander with great will-power and iron resistance could have survived.

Despite the new lustre which the expedition had given to the name of De Wet, the invasion was a failure. Had he not been hampered by swollen rivers,

De Wet would doubtless have been able to penetrate deeper into the Cape Colony and in so doing would presumably have brought considerable relief to the commandos in the Free State and the Transvaal, but realistically this would not have made any difference to the eventual outcome of the war.

EASTERN TRANSVAAL

A quiet period

After the battle of Dalmanutha there was a period of comparative quiet in the eastern parts of the Transvaal. Initially there were no major clashes. For the most part, Botha was busy north of the the railway line to Delagoa Bay. To the south of the railway the commandos were all operating in their own districts but because the British still had a numerically superior force, confrontations were avoided if at all possible.

The British did their best to catch the commandos but achieved little success. British columns were moving around all over the Highveld to try to clear the region of republican forces, but their efforts were in vain because time and again the commandos managed to give them the slip.

The only clashes of significance in the eastern part of the Transvaal before the end of 1900 took place under the direction of General Ben Viljoen. The first of these was on 29 November in the Bushveld north of Pretoria where a column under General A.H. Paget came up against Viljoen's commando. It was a hard fought encounter which left the British with heavy losses, but their superior numbers told in the end and Viljoen judged it best to retreat under cover of darkness.

A month later, on 29 December, Viljoen made up for the setback at Renosterkop. He and General C.H. Muller set their sights on an isolated British column at Helvetia near Machadodorp. The British camp was attacked at night from two directions and before the soldiers realised fully what was happening, they were overwhelmed.

On this occasion the large cannon named after Lady Roberts was captured by the republican forces. This inspired F.W. Reitz to write a poem which is still widely read today. The defeat at Helvetia was a harsh reminder to the British that the fighting spirit among the commandos was still alive and well.

A new spirit in the resistance

The year 1901 brought a sudden change in the comparative calm. Once he had completed a thorough reorganisation of the commandos, Botha began to look around for a suitable opportunity to take on his opponents again. He decided to attack the British garrisons that were stationed along the Delagoa Bay railway.

After Botha had consulted with Viljoen, he launched a series of attacks on Belfast, Machadodorp, Panstasie, Wonderfontein and a number of smaller places along the railway on the night of 7 January 1901.

The most important clash was at Belfast. Although initially the Boers managed to capture a few British forts, the attack failed in the end because the misty weather frustrated attempts at cooperation among the various commandos. The British garrisons at all the other stations were on their guard and again the weather favoured them, with the result that all the Boer attacks were repulsed.

WESTERN TRANSVAAL

Nooitgedacht

In the western districts of the Transvaal after September 1900 there was also a comparatively calm period. Sporadic skirmishes occurred but they were of little significance. De la Rey made use of the opportunity, with the assistance of General J.C. Smuts, to undertake a thorough reorganisation of the commandos.

In November De la Rey was ready to take on the enemy again. He had his sights set on the columns under Major-General Clements who was in the Magaliesberg Mountains between Rustenburg and Krugersdorp. These columns were somewhat isolated and an attack on them had a fairly good chance of succeeding. De la Rey decided to tackle Clements in cooperation with Beyers, who was encamped at Warmbaths at the time. Beyers moved in great secrecy towards the west and joined De la Rey a few days later.

The British had camped at the foot of the Magaliesberg Mountains and high up on the summit Clements had built a series of stone forts. It was decided that De la Rey would attack the camp while Beyers and his men would storm the forts. Early on the morning of 13 December the attack was launched. Relatively seldom has a burgher attack been carried out with such utter fearlessness. Beyers was without doubt the best man to spur on the burghers to climb the steep sides of the mountain and to storm the forts. Meanwhile De la Rey's men attacked the camp but were unable to make much headway. When Beyers and his burghers also began to bombard the enemy from the top of the mountain, there was no stopping the British: they took to their heels and left the entire camp in the hands of the Boers.

This battle, known as Nooitgedacht, was one of the most brilliant victories gained by the republican forces in the war.

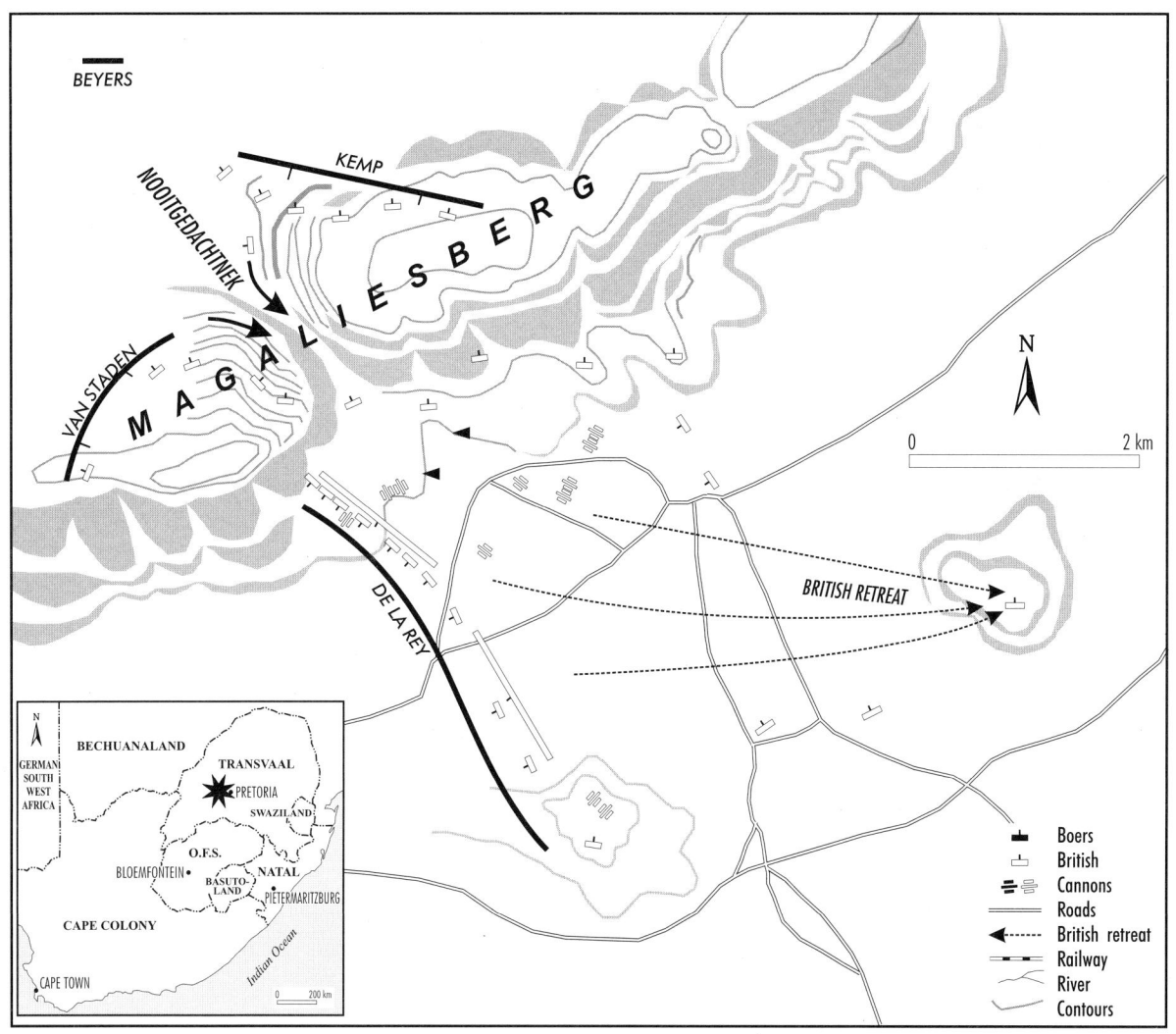

Nooitgedacht, 13 December 1900

87

Renewed resistance

The victory at Nooitgedacht had a very favourable effect on the morale of the Transvaal burghers, giving them a resurgence of enthusiasm. In more than one respect, Nooitgedacht was also the prelude to a great renewal of the struggle in the western Transvaal.

The commandos under De la Rey and Beyers did not delay for long in the Magaliesberg region because strong British forces were sent to exact revenge for the defeat. At this stage the two generals parted company and Beyers soon managed to get behind the British. He then undertook the daring feat of crossing the railway between Pretoria and Johannesburg and thus went into the eastern part of the Transvaal.

CHAPTER VIII
THE SCORCHED EARTH POLICY

THE BEGINNING OF 1901

Kitchener's decision

When Kitchener took over the supreme command of the British forces at the end of November 1900, the guerrilla phase of the war had only just begun. The reawakening of resistance in all parts of the two republics was thus an unpleasant shock to him, particularly as his predecessor, Roberts, had been of the opinion that the war was over. Furthermore the victories gained by the republican forces before the end of 1900 had been difficult for the British to accept. It became clear to Kitchener and his subordinates that something had to be done to make it impossible for the Boers to continue their guerrilla tactics.

The decision taken by Kitchener was implemented early in 1901. The new strategy comprised three measures. Firstly, the two republics were subjected to systematic devastation as experienced by very few other countries in the world. Towns were completely burned down. In some places even the churches were destroyed. In the countryside all Boer homes were totally demolished or burned to the ground. All supplies of food such as grain or mealies were destroyed. Cattle which could not be led away were killed. In a nutshell, within a few months the Transvaal and Free State were reduced to a vast wilderness where food could not be found for man or beast.

Secondly, all the women and children were put into concentration camps.

Thirdly, the British forces now launched five great drives, aimed to trap the commandos. Along the railway lines or between specific towns, they built lines of blockhouses. A small division of soldiers was placed in each blockhouse to

Lord Kitchener

A British blockhouse

stop the commandos from passing through. The British columns, which formed a continuous closed line over long distances, then began to drive the commandos in the direction of the block-houses. The commandos would thus find them-selves, as it were, in an enclosure from which they would be unable to escape and this would force them to surrender. To implement this strategy Kitchener changed to using horsemen only because foot soldiers were unsuited to this new type of warfare.

Kitchener predicted that when the commandos could no longer find any means of sustenance, when the women and children of the burghers on commando were all in camps, and when the commandos were being mercilessly chased around, the end of the war and the complete subjugation of the two republics would soon follow.

The concentration camps

Concentration camps were first set up early in 1901. Thousands of women and children who were still living in the towns and on farms at this stage of the war were evacuated from their homes, often by force, with little opportunity for taking more than a few items of clothing or blankets with them. They were then transported in ox wagons or in open railway carriages to camps that had been specially set up to house captured women and children.

The camps were usually tents that had been pitched in the open veld and the inmates were almost completely exposed to the elements. In the summer it was unbearably hot in the tents, while in the winter they offered little protection against the cold and the wind. Large families were often housed in a single tent. The British authorities were not equipped to provide the necessary food for the many thousands of women and children who had been sent to the camps and the rations that were distributed were completely inadequate, in many respects, so the inmates often went hungry. This had a very debilitating effect on the resistance of the children, particularly the younger ones, making them susceptible to all kinds of disease. Many illnesses suddenly made their appearance in the concentration camps and

Concentration camp at Norvalspont

the death rate increased. In total, more than 26 000 women and children died in the camps as a result of starvation and disease. For the small Afrikaner nation, the death of so many thousands of people was an overwhelming loss.

The *Vrouemonument* (Women's Memorial) at Bloemfontein was erected in remembrance of the women and children who died in the camps.

The treatment that the women and children received in the camps did not carry the approval of the British public as a whole. An influential group often expressed sharp criticism on the government's military policy. A British woman, Emily Hobhouse, came to South Africa specially to visit the concentration camps and the disclosures that she made ultimately led to a slight improvement of camp conditions.

The National Scouts and Africans in the war

Before a description is given of the military action that took place during 1901, it is necessary to mention something which occurred in this period: the formation of the National Scouts. They were republican burghers who defected to the British and fought on their side. According to British records there were approximately 4 000 National Scouts at the end of the war. The particular value of these men to the British was their knowledge of the military tactics of the commandos which made them far better than the British at devising counter measures.

91

Emily Hobhouse

It was, for example, the National Scouts who taught the British how to make night raids on sleeping commandos and burghers and in this way many men were killed or taken prisoner. The National Scouts also often acted as convoy guards, because they were far better at handling animals than the British soldiers. The use of National Scouts caused great bitterness among those burghers who were still fighting for the Boer cause.

Even greater embitterment resulted when the British military commanders made use of armed Africans. An armed black man was usually shot by the Boers if he was caught, because it was their view that Africans should not become involved in a war between white people.

Kitchener's first great drive

The Transvaal Highveld was the first part of the two republics that Kitchener chose for the implementation of his new strategy. A strong force of 15 000 men and 63 cannons under the leadership of French was deployed to the east of the Witwatersrand. This force, which was joined from time to time by other columns, was given orders to carry out the systematic destruction of the entire region between the railway lines to Delagoa Bay and Durban. The aim was to leave behind nothing that could be of any use to the commandos. The commandos themselves were then to be surrounded and forced to surrender. All women and children were to be captured and transported elsewhere.

On 28 January 1901 the British columns which stretched from Pretoria to Heidelberg began their march. They were to move in close formation so that no commando would stand a chance of slipping through the net. The republican forces were caught unawares by this new strategy. Everywhere they came up against overwhelming numbers so that there was no chance to resist. Small divisions of burghers did nevertheless succeed in slipping through the enemy lines and thus got behind the British where they were safe for a time, although there was nothing left on which to survive. Shortly after French's men had set off, they were joined by a second force stretching from Balmoral to Middelburg. In this wide arc they moved towards Ermelo.

Botha found himself pitted against this massive force with a mere 2 000 burghers. A man of his calibre was not going to allow himself to be trapped in this way, and he waited for an opportunity to break through the British lines and reach safety.

While a British column was fast asleep on the night of 6 February at Chrissiesmeer, they were rudely awakened by Botha. The attack was not a resounding success because the commandos found it difficult to communicate efficiently in the dark and although the enemy had heavy losses, Botha's men also suffered gravely. But at least Botha had escaped from the threat of encirclement.

The British columns then continued their march in the direction of Piet Retief, Vryheid and Utrecht until they reached the border of Natal at the beginning of April.

A large part of the Transvaal now lay in ash and ruins. Almost all the Boer homesteads had been burned and the cattle slaughtered or taken as booty, and all the women and children had been sent to the concentration camps. The Highveld was little more than a wilderness and there was practically no means of subsistence for the commandos. And every day the winter drew nearer.

Peace negotiations

Kitchener thought that by following his new strategy he would soon bring the republican leaders to the realisation that further resistance was useless and that they should simply submit themselves to the authority of Britain. He thought that perhaps the matter of concluding peace could be speeded up by negotiating with Botha.

On 28 February the two commanders met for talks at Middelburg. Kitchener told Botha that the two republics had to sacrifice their independence and become British colonies.

Certain rights would however be extended to the Afrikaners such as the use of their language in schools and the courts. A measure of compensation would be paid for the damage caused by the British forces to the private property of burghers. After a few years, a limited form of self-government would be granted to the two colonies. Africans would not be given the franchise.

A bridge built by the Boer forces

Botha found these conditions unacceptable and turned them down, which meant that the war would be continued.

THE WINTER OF 1901

The destruction continues

The devastation endured on the Transvaal Highveld in the last months of the summer of 1901 soon struck the other parts of the two republics too. It was a systematic destruction such as few countries of the world have ever known. When the winter of 1901 finally arrived, there was a scene of utter desolation stretching from north of the Orange River to the Limpopo. Hardly a single Boer homestead had been left unscathed and there were neither people nor animals. Laagers of women moved around in a desperate attempt to stay out of the hands of the British forces. In short, during the winter months scenes of the greatest hardship and misery were seen throughout the two republics.

Kitchener's strategy obviously had a very detrimental influence on the well-being of the republican forces. There was no more food for the burghers because everything on the farms had been destroyed. The people could no longer sustain themselves because they had lost everything. Rifles and ammunition were no longer readily available. In such dire circumstances the commandos were obliged to live off the enemy. Each commando waited for an opportunity to attack a British column and force it to surrender.

When the white flag was raised the burghers plundered the enemy soldiers, taking their food supplies. Rifles and ammunition were taken and then used by the Boers against the enemy. By the end of the war most of the burghers were using the same weapons and ammunition as the British. Horses were also plundered, as were shoes, riding breeches, shirts and jackets – anything in fact that could be used to protect the body against wind and weather. When this process of *uitskud* (literally "shaking out"), as it was called, was over the British usually looked pretty dismal. As the Boers could no longer take any prisoners of war, the soldiers were later set free and allowed to return to their comrades.

Although the commandos still accomplished feats of great bravery, it was clear that the scorched earth policy was turning the tide against them. The result was that their military activities diminished during the winter months.

War weariness

To cling to the belief of eventual victory while suffering under such dire circumstances called for men with an unflinching, iron will. Not everyone is blessed with these qualities and so it is perhaps understandable that there were also men who began to doubt whether the war should continue. One such man was the Acting President Schalk Burger of the Transvaal Republic who headed the government after the departure of Kruger in September 1900.

Burger and other members of the Transvaal government were of the opinion that the war should be called off and that negotiations should be held with the enemy. It was on their initiative that a letter in this vein was sent to the Free State government on 10 May.

This letter made a very poor impression on Steyn and he suggested that the members of the two governments should meet one another to discuss the situation. Steyn decided to take De Wet with him and De la Rey, who had come from the western Transvaal, would also accompany them. The meeting between the two governments took place on 20 June in the Standerton district. Steyn's opinion was upheld and it was decided that the war should continue until Britain was prepared to recognise the independence of the two republics. To bring some much needed relief to the republics it was agreed that a new attack would be launched into the Cape Colony. This time it would be led by Smuts.

Steyn and De Wet then returned to the Free State, while De la Rey found his way back to the western Transvaal. On 11 July Steyn narrowly escaped an early morning British attack at Reitz. A number of members of the Free State government as well as Steyn's correspondence — including the letter from the Transvaal government — fell into enemy hands. Kitchener thus had the proof that his scorched earth strategy was having the desired effect. He only had to maintain the policy and victory would eventually be his.

It was reading the letter from the Transvaal government that moved Kitchener to issue a proclamation threatening that those burghers who refused to lay down their arms would be bannned from South Africa and their possessions confiscated. The proclamation had no effect at all.

THE STRUGGLE IS CONTINUED

The Cape Colony

It has already been shown that Hertzog, Kritzinger and Scheepers succeeded in invading the Cape in December 1900. Hertzog returned to the Free State in February 1901 together with De Wet, but Kritzinger and Scheepers had remained behind in the Cape Colony to continue the resistance against the British. Their example was soon to be followed by more burghers.

Within the first months of 1901 the commandos under men such as Commandant W.D. Fouché, General H.W. Lategan, General W.C. Malan, Commandant D.J.S. Theron, General S.G. Maritz and others, also managed to cross the Orange River and move into the Cape Colony.

A commando of this nature seldom comprises more than a hundred men. A considerable number of Cape Afrikaners once again joined the republican forces. The commandos' most important objective was to cut off the British communications with the north and to draw as many troops as possible out of the republics and into the Cape Colony. In this they were extremely successful.

The commandos caused so much havoc in the Cape that by May 1901 Kitchener was obliged to send French there with orders to destroy them. French, who had his headquarters at Middelburg (Transvaal), had 50 000 men under him. In comparison, the commandos at that stage probably numbered no more than 3 000 men.

The Cape Colony covers an extremely large area and is very mountainous. This afforded the commandos many opportunities to move around and when the numerically superior British force made matters too hot for them, they could always find refuge in the mountains, where they could seldom be trapped. The fighting raged from Aliwal North in the east to Port Nolloth in the west and from Philipstown in the north to the vicinity of Cape Town in the south. The nature of the encounters in the Cape was such that there were no major battles, nevertheless the fact that so many thousands of British soldiers had been drawn into the Cape Colony meant a great deal to the two republics.

The Free State

In the Free State the winter months of 1901 brought additional desolation to the destruction that had been caused by the roving British columns. As the days passed the commandos found less and less to eat, so they avoided large skirmishes wherever possible. Their main goal was to survive the winter, and as soon as the first spring rains fell they would renew their efforts. Only when a real opportunity presented itself did the burghers attack the enemy and take possession of whatever useful goods they could find.

The Transvaal

In the Transvaal there was more or less the same situation as in the Free State. The destruction of so many private homes certainly hampered the commandos in their military operations. Here too the main objective was to get through the harsh winter months and to try to come up with a new military initiative with the onset of spring.

Nevertheless a few encounters took place in the winter months, most of which ended in favour of the Boers. They were evidence that the war was by no means over.

It is necessary to refer to only two of the battles that occurred during the winter. Both were significant because they were waged by men who began the war as ordinary burghers, but were promoted to the rank of general in 1901 after showing extraordinary bravery and military expertise. They were General J.C.G. Kemp and General C.H. Muller.

The first of these battles, in which Kemp was involved, took place on 30 May at Vlakfontein near Swartruggens. Here for the first time he applied a new strategy which later led to a number of republican victories: attacking a British column while it was on the march.

When a column was on the move, the advance guard and rearguard were often a few miles apart. If a quick charge was made the column could be severely punished before the British troops could close their ranks.

Kemp's eye fell on the column headed by General Dixon. Under cover of a veld fire that had broken out, the Boers attacked the troops at the rear of the moving British column, inflicted heavy losses and even captured a few cannons.

The rest of the column, which had not yet taken part in the fighting, then launched a counter-attack and eventually managed to recapture the cannons.

Despite the fact that the Boers were forced to leave the battlefield, Dixons's position was so desperate that he thought it wise to see if he could find some security by joining other stronger British units.

The second clash involved Muller and took place on 12 June at Wilmansrust between Middelburg and Ermelo. A British division made up of Australian volunteers and under the leadership of Major Morris was separated from the other columns which were making a charge over the Highveld. Muller decide to make good use of the situation.

While the Australians were getting ready to enjoy their dinner, the Boers, who had come to within about eighteen metres of the camp, suddenly opened fierce fire on them out of the darkness. The enemy was taken so completely by surprise that there was simply no chance of any resistance. After plundering two cannons, many horses and large quantities of supplies, Muller disappeared just as silently as he had arrived.

Before concluding, another piece of information on the struggle in the Transvaal in the winter of 1901 should be mentioned. It has already been noted that at the meeting between the two republican governments near Standerton it was decided to send more commandos to the Cape Colony. This task was to be carried out by Smuts who was originally under De la Rey in the western Transvaal.

On 15 July Smuts with barely 350 men set off from the Potchefstroom area on the long journey. It was an extremely adventurous undertaking because right from the beginning they were halted time and time again by British columns in long lines carrying out military drives on the Free State plains. The little commandos which were always in danger of being caught then had to try to evade the enemy by making night marches. In this they were successful and eventually, on 27 August, Smuts and 250 men reached Zastron in the southern Free State. On 3 September he was able to cross the Orange River without being stopped by the British, and he moved into the Cape Colony.

CHAPTER IX
THE LAST PHASE OF THE WAR

The circumstances that prevailed in the winter months of 1901 meant that the republican forces had to go on the defence as much as possible. However, the spring had barely arrived when there was a general feeling of euphoria. It was felt that the British military commanders should be made to realise that the burghers would not yield and were certainly not planning to give up the struggle. This was the Boer reply to Kitchener's proclamation that threatened them with banning and confiscation of their property if they refused to lay down their arms before 15 September.

In September the theatre of war stretched from the vicinity of Cape Town in the south to the Limpopo in the north and from the Mozambican border in the east to the border of South West Africa (now Namibia), which was a German colony at the time, in the west. A large number of British columns were moving around in this vast area in a vain attempt to break the resistance of the Boer commandos. When the slightest opportunity presented itself, the commandos would swoop down on the enemy and deal them a swift punch. Steyn still hoped that if the resistance could just hold on for long enough, the British public would eventually grow weary of the war and would force the government to declare peace with the recognition of republican independence.

THE CAPE COLONY

The arrival of Smuts

When Smuts succeeded in crossing the Orange River the war in the Cape Colony entered a new phase. He was in effect at the head of all the commandos. The task that awaited him was certainly not an easy one; the British were keen to capture him because this would make it so much easier to handle the resistance in the Cape Colony. For this reason strong British columns constantly harassed the Smuts commando and it was only due to great persistence and endurance that time and again they succeeded in escaping from the British attempts at encirclement. First Smuts spread out in the direction of the eastern Cape. After a series of narrow escapes he moved towards the south-western districts. The enemy hardly ever left him in peace, but they were nevertheless unable to prevent him from moving exactly where he wanted to go. Near Oudtshoorn Smuts began to turn north, hoping to reach the north-western districts. He arrived there early in January 1902 and met up with the commando under Maritz.

Maritz, who had been moving around with his commando since the beginning of 1901, had also caused the British a great deal of trouble. He was a fearless fighter and had even taken the risk of venturing into the western Cape in the last months of 1901. It was a source of concern to the British army authorities that the commandos dared to go as far south as Piketberg and Ceres. Small divisions were in the very shadow of Table Mountain and a skirmish had even taken place between the two opposing parties at Darling, a few kilometres from Cape Town.

Once Smuts and Maritz had joined forces they could even risk going strongly on the attack. In March 1902 they succeeded in taking Springbok. They then besieged Okiep, but when a large British force approached they thought it wise to back off.

Other commanders also made things difficult for the British in the Cape Colony in the final stage of the war. One of the best known of these was Commandant G.J. (Gideon) Scheepers, a young man of 22 years of age. After delaying for a while in the vicinity of Graaff-Reinet, he moved further south.

Near Ladismith he became so seriously ill that his men had to leave him behind in the hands of the British. He was then taken to Graaff-Reinet where he stood trial before a military court, was found guilty of contravening military law and condemned to death. The sentence was carried out on 22 January. It is sufficient to point out here that Scheepers denied being guilty of the deeds of which he was accused.

Kritzinger, the man who had crossed the Orange River with Scheepers in December 1900, was also destined to fall into British hands. He was seriously wounded in a clash and had to be left on the battlefield, where he was taken prisoner by the British.

The same fate was to befall another commander, General Wynand Malan. While launching an attack on a British division he was seriously wounded and was also captured by the British.

Although commandos from north of the Orange River succeeded in invading the Cape Colony time and again during the course of 1901, it would have been very difficult for them had they not had help from the Cape Afrikaners. Almost everywhere the invading commandos could reckon on a friendly and hospitable reception. Of greater significance was the fact that a considerable number of Afrikaners joined the commandos. Among these Cape rebels were some of the bravest campaigners for republican independence.

British countermeasures

The sympathy and support which the invading commandos enjoyed at the hands of the Cape Afrikaners caused many a headache for the British miltary commanders. They decided they should take every possible military measure to restrict this support. Martial law was declared for the entire Cape Colony and all forms of communication were halted. The majority of horses, wagons and carts were removed from the Boer farms so that the commandos could not make use of them. Even the slightest show of sympathy for the republican cause was heavily punished.

It goes without saying that the Cape Afrikaners who recieved the heaviest censure were those who had taken up arms for the republics. They were British subjects and by joining the republican forces they had become rebels. The British military authorities were very concerned that the rebellion would become widespread because it was clear that if the majority of the Cape Afrikaners rebelled, the position of the British forces in South Africa would become extremely critical. It was this consideration that made Kitchener decide to use strong measures to discourage the Afrikaners from rebelling.

The most important of these measures was the death penalty. Some offenders were sentenced to imprisonment.

Although the action taken by the British military authorities certainly discouraged more than one Cape Afrikaner from throwing in his lot with his fellow republicans, Kitchener did not achieve his goal. Right up until the end of the war there were still Cape Afrikaners who joined the commandos when the opportunity arose and who fought for the maintenance of republican independence.

THE FREE STATE

The spring brings revival

The arrival of the spring rejuvenated the commandos in the Free State and spurred them to new action. Because the British still had a numerically superior force it was unwise to engage in any large scale conflict. The strategy adopted by De Wet and his subordinates was now primarily one of starting only small skirmishes. If a weak British division became separated in any way, it was immediately attacked and more than likely destroyed. The resistance in the Free State during the last months of 1901 was characterised by many of these skirmishes which almost always ended in favour of the Boers. Winning these clashes was now the only way in which the commandos could get the supplies they needed to continue the war. The most important of these smaller clashes was certainly the one at Tafelkop between Frankfort and Vrede where, on 20 December, General W.J. Wessels managed to practically wipe out the columns under Colonel Damant.

Needless to say, by suffering these defeats the British forces were indeed somewhat constrained, but this did not prevent them from continuing their campaign of destruction in the Free State.

Groenkop (Tweefontein)

Because it was almost impossible for him to deploy a large number of burghers at a specific point, De Wet also found it difficult to gain decisive victories over his opponents. He was forced to wait for a good opportunity. Such an opportunity presented itself a week before Christmas when a British column set up camp at Groenkop between Bethlehem and Harrismith. On the eastern side this hill slopes gradually down into the surrounding plains. In the west, however, it rises well above the level of the plains and is very steep indeed. On the eastern side the British had constructed a number of entrenchments to protect them from possible attack. They had decided that no enemy would ever dare to climb the steep cliffs on the western side, so they had not put up any defences there.

This fact had not escaped the eagle eye of De Wet and he now decided that the opportunity he had awaited for so long had at last arrived. His burghers would take the British by surprise and would climb the steep cliffs of Groenkop at the dead of night. Silently, while the British soldiers were fast asleep, De Wet's men approached the foot of the hill. The few guards who were keeping watch were simply shot and then the burghers quickly scaled the steep sides of the peak. The first burghers were at the top before most of the British realised what was happening. Many of them were killed or wounded in the places where they lay sleeping. Among those killed was Major Williams, their commander. In such circumstances, resistance was out of the question.

On the British side there were almost 150 wounded or killed, while De Wet's losses were comparatively light. The burghers also found a great deal of booty in the British camp.

New drives to catch De Wet

De Wet's victory at Groenkop was a real blow to the British army command, so Kitchener decided that more blockhouses would have to be built to restrict the movements of the commandos. The entire area along the railway line to Johannesburg and the Drakensberg Mountains was soon dotted with many lines of blockhouses designed to keep the enemy out of certain areas and to trap the commandos when there was a military drive against them. To make escape even more difficult, barbed wire was strung between the blockhouses making it almost impossible for a mounted burgher to get through.

Kitchener was determined to catch De Wet. If this man were to fall into British hands the resistance in the Free State would immediately crumble. This was the British reasoning. During the first weeks of 1902 they concentrated their entire effort on catching De Wet. Strong British forces under the most skilled commanders were deployed in the northern parts of the Free State.

These forces were to move in a crescent formation in order to drive De Wet and his burghers up against the blockhouses where he would be forced to surrender. They planned to use more than 30 000 soldiers for this purpose, while De Wet did not have more than 2 000 men at any stage of this campaign.

A destroyed bridge

The first attempt to neutralise De Wet once and for all was a drive comprising a large number of columns stretching from Frankfort to Lindley which would march towards the railway line to Johannesburg. The garrisons in the blockhouses along this railway line were strengthened considerably to make sure that De Wet would not be able to break through. On 6 February the British forces started moving forward. The intention was that the columns should reach the railway line after three or four days, so that the Boers would have very little chance of escaping.

The ever-alert De Wet soon realised what the British were planning to do. He marshalled his troops very quickly and on the night of 7 February he broke through the blockhouse line between Lindley and Kroonstad with comparative ease. He then went south to Doringberg to reach safety.

The first British attempt to catch De Wet thus ended in failure and afterwards the commandos returned to their various districts. This immediately made Kitchener decide to organise a second, even bigger hunt for De Wet. The plan was to clear the commandos from the entire region between the railway line to Johannesburg from Durban, the Drakensberg and a line stretching from Doringberg to Harrismith. Columns from all sides would draw even closer together to prevent the Boers from escaping again. As a result of this effort many Free State commandos ran into trouble because they were always hopelessly outnumbered and usually had to retreat– only to move deeper into the large enclosure the British were creating.

De Wet showed once again that he had no equal as a guerrilla leader. His scouts kept him well informed of the British movements so that he was able to plan his umpteenth escape. On the night of 23 February with a few hundred burghers he made a surprise attack on the British at Holspruit in the Vrede district and simply crushed all resistance. When the sun rose the next morning De Wet and Steyn, who was with him, were safely beyond the reach of the British columns.

Kitchener then organised a third attempt to capture De Wet. On 4 March a new drive was launched to push the commandos in the northern part of the Free State against the line of blockhouses along the railway line to Johannesburg.

This attempt was also an abject failure because not only did Steyn and De Wet find their way to the western part of the Free State, but other commandos also managed to break out of the British encirclement with reasonable ease. This marked the end of the conflict in the Free State during the early summer months of 1902.

EASTERN TRANSVAAL

An unsuccessful attempt to invade Natal

The winter of 1901 on the cold, devastated Highveld had forced Botha into a period of inactivity, but when the spring months arrived he felt the need to show the British that the war in the eastern Transvaal was far from over and that the commandos under him still had plenty of striking power. The air early in September was still thin and sharp when the first spring rains began to fall softly down onto the scorched, blackened Highveld. The change in the weather also inspired the commandos to pick themselves up.

Botha decided to invade Natal again so as to lure a number of British columns out of the Transvaal. It appears that by August the British might well have got wind of his plan because they began to take a number of steps to counteract such an attack. Strong British forces were soon placed along the Natal border to prevent a possible invasion. Botha and his commandos meanwhile set off on their journey southwards on 5 September.

As soon as the British heard about this, strong columns were sent in pursuit so that Botha now had the enemy both ahead of him and at his rear. Luckily for Botha the British forces did not succeed in catching up with him because Botha's manoeuvres had misled them completely. Only once, on 17 September at Scheepersnek, did a British force cross Botha's path. The result was a heavy British defeat. On this occasion Botha employed a new military tactic for the first time: he used his mounted burghers to make attacking charges and the end result was one which the enemy certainly did not enjoy.

Botha now rapidly approached the Natal border. He had only 2 000 men and he was faced by a British force of 16 000.

General Botha's invasion of Natal

Two British forts, Itala and Prospect, lay in his path on his southwards march. Botha thought it wise to try to defeat them before he went further south. On the night of 25 September his commandos attacked the forts. The defence by the garrisons was very courageous and as morning broke it was clear that the Boers had lost many men. In addition the columns behind the commandos were now quickly closing in.

Under these circumstances Botha had only one way open to him if he was to avoid being trapped: he had to stop the attacks, abandon the

107

General Louis Botha

plan to invade Natal, and move out of reach of the enemy. His evasion of the columns was successful and by the beginning of October he and all his commandos were back on the Highveld.

Bakenlaagte

Fairly soon afterwards Botha was able to make up for the reverse he had suffered by achieving a brilliant victory. Previously, British columns had operated on the Highveld under Colonel Benson, an extremely capable commander who had apparently caused the commandos more trouble than anyone else. Circumstances were such that at the end of October Benson's columns had become completely detached from the others. Furthermore, Benson had decided to move from Middelburg (Transvaal) to Bethal.

It did not escape Botha's attention that Benson's columns were alone on the Highveld. His dispatch riders sped off to round up all the nearby commandos for an attack on the moving British columns. In no time at all the commandos met at the appointed place. Botha was to take the lead personally.

On the morning of 30 October, when he wanted to continue his march, Benson noticed that he was up against a considerable number of commandos. He thought that he would be able to shake them off easily, but this certainly did not happen.

By midday more commandos arrived and Botha then decided to go onto the attack immediately. In pouring rain the mounted Boers stormed the rearguard of Benson's force. The soldiers, led by Benson himself, took up a defensive position on a ridge, but against the storming burghers, who were firing from the saddle, they had little chance. It was an assault second to none. Hardly a single soldier survived the carnage. Benson was mortally wounded and died that same evening. Two cannons also

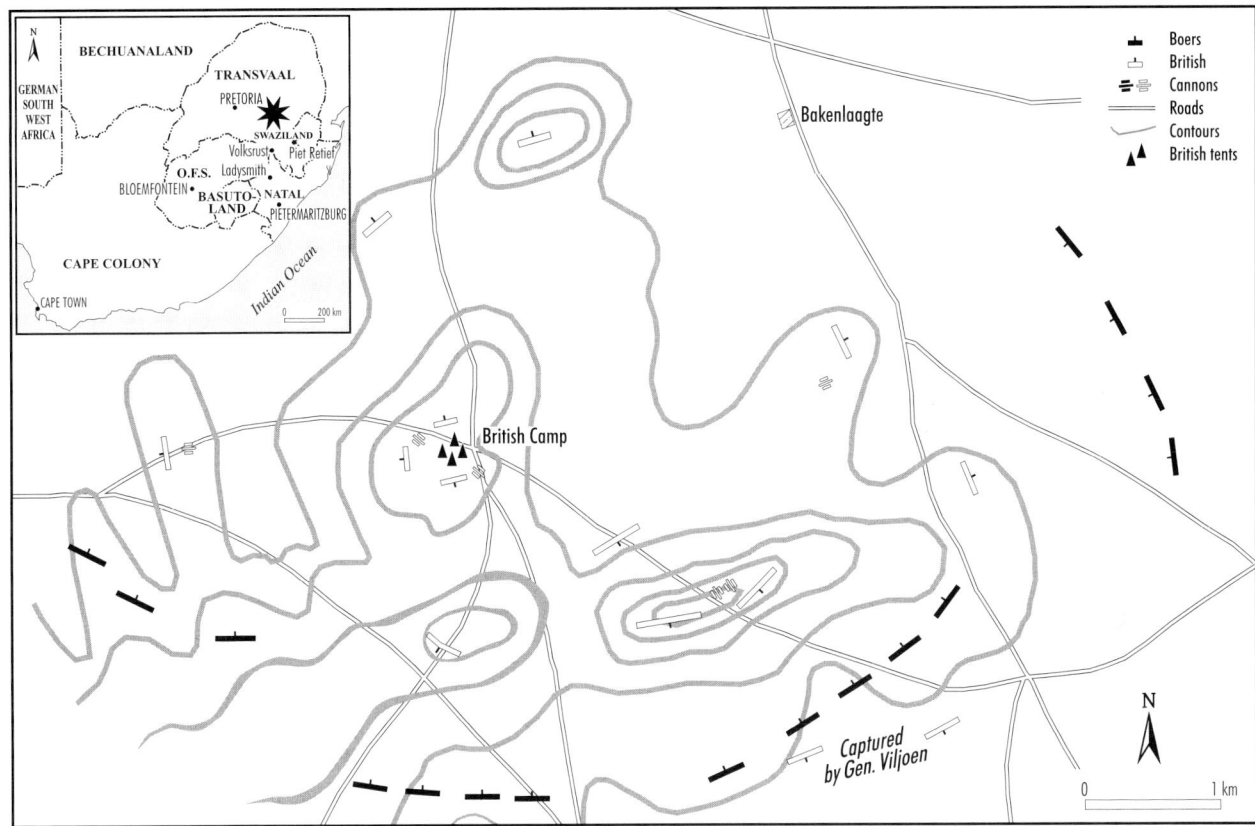

Bakenlaagte, 30 October 1901

fell into Boer hands. The victory won, Botha and his commandos disbanded once again. It was the end of the line for the British column that had caused so much trouble.

The ongoing course of the war

After the battle of Bakenlaagte the war in the eastern part of the Transvaal was not characterised by any other major encounters. Small skirmishes took place everywhere but they were not of any consequence in the course of the war. The British army command set great store on hunting Botha down. They would have liked to have caught him but were never able to do so.

They had more success with General B.J. (Ben) Viljoen. He was captured by a British division in January 1902 while he was on a night march with a few of his officers.

109

General Koos de la Rey

WESTERN TRANSVAAL

Moedwil

The arrival of the spring of 1901 caused a burst of activity in the western Transvaal commandos that was unequalled anywhere else. It was here that De la Rey was able to build up a select band, a fighting force that he planned to use to good effect against the enemy.

The first encounter of note that took place in this part of the battle zone was on 30 September at Moedwil between Rustenburg and Zeerust. Kekewich, the man who had previously defended Kimberley with such success, was encamped here with a strong column. De la Rey decided to attack the British camp which was on the banks of the Selons River. He quickly drew up his commandos and aided by the wooded terrain he was able to get very close to the enemy camp. De la Rey divided his burghers into four groups. Two had to fire on the camp itself while the other two had to attack the flanks of the British force.

In the twilight the Boers suddenly opened a fierce barrage of fire on the sleeping soldiers in the camp. Despite the initial confusion, the discipline among the soldiers was very good. They reacted promptly to the orders issued by Kekewich, who was himself wounded twice. In comparison, the cooperation between the different groups of burghers was not very satisfactory. The result was that although the British suffered heavy losses, De la Rey was unable to capture the camp. The British defence was too strong and after the clash had raged for more than an hour, De la Rey was forced to call back his commandos and withdraw.

Driefontein (Kleinfontein)

Every now and then the wandering British columns gave De la Rey the chance he was waiting for and he was able to attack them. Such an opportunity arose when the column of Colonel Von Donop was on the move from Mafeking to Zeerust. On 24 October, while the British were slowly threading their way through the bush with a large number of wagons, they were suddenly attacked by De la Rey's burghers. The tactics used at Vlakfontein were employed again. While a division of burghers kept the British vanguard busy, another group under the command of Kemp attacked the centre and quickly overwhelmed it. Twelve wagons were plundered and removed.

Two of the gunners were shot dead at their cannons, but because the horses were still being used in the fight, the cannons could not be removed and were later reclaimed by the British. Von Donop had offered stout resistance and since the Boers had also suffered heavily, they were forced to retreat. The encounter certainly showed that the British had a very dangerous opponent in De la Rey.

Ysterspruit

Following the clash at Driefontien the war in the western Transvaal went into a quiet period which was broken only in February 1902. Once again the British gave De la Rey the opportunity to deal them a heavy blow. A large column was moving from Wolmaransstad to Klerksdorp. De la Rey needed ammunition and he thought that it would be a good idea to get it from the enemy. Before sunrise on the morning of 25 February the column under the leadership of Anderson began its march because the soldiers were hoping to reach Klerksdorp the same day.

They would not succeed in doing so, because they had gone no more than a few kilometres when the burghers launched their attack. General P.J. Liebenberg attacked the vanguard, while General Kemp took on the centre and General J.G.Celliers went for the rear. Initially the British defence was so solid that Liebenberg and Kemp made little progress. But Celliers stormed in so courageously with his horsemen that the British soldiers at the rear succumbed.

This was the beginning of the end. Although Anderson made another valiant attempt to escape, he failed to do so and, having sustained great losses, the whole column fell into De la Rey's hands. He now had more than enough ammunition to last for a very long time.

Lord Methuen

Tweebosch

The defeat at Ysterspruit was a bitter blow to the British, but they were unaware that a more serious reverse awaited them. This time De la Rey's victim was none other than Methuen, second in command after Kitchener. Methuen planned to move his column from Vryburg to Klerksdorp so that he could dispose of De la Rey. The Boer general, who was well informed of every move the British made, was for his part just as anxious to get the better of the enemy again.

Methuen and his column camped at Tweebosch on the night of 6 March. He planned to get under way again early the next morning. The British were barely on the move when their rearguard was suddenly attacked by De la Rey's burghers. Methuen promptly strengthened his rearguard and this was exactly what De la Rey had been waiting for. Other divisions which he had held back until this moment now moved in on the rest of the column, causing total disarray in the British ranks. The mounted burghers stormed the enemy and those who were able to do so simply took to their heels. Methuen himself bravely tried to rescue the situation, but he suffered a leg injury and fell into Boer hands. De la Rey was compassionate enough to send him to Klerksdorp where he could be treated by his own doctor.

Tweebosch was the most brilliant of all De la Rey's victories.

Rooiwal (near the Harts River)

Despite their success at Tweebosch, the war in the western Transvaal ended in a serious defeat for the republican forces. The British wanted to avenge the two reverses inflicted upon them by De la Rey and so in the second half of March 1902 they deployed a very large force in the western Transvaal. On 11 April at Rooiwal near the Harts River the British got the opportunity they had been waiting for. At the time De la Rey was in Klerksdorp where the two republican governments, as will be seen in the next chapter, had met to discuss peace. Kemp had taken command of the commandos and, faced by the combined forces under

Grenfell, Kekewich and Von Donop, he decided to go on the attack. Because these columns were not on the march they were not spread out over a wide area.

The British soldiers on the side of a ridge were in a strong position and the burghers had to cover a fair distance on their horses in order to storm them. Kemp's attempt was a brave one, but it was doomed to failure because the British used their advantage to deadly effect, inflicting heavy losses on their exposed attackers.

The burghers got to within 300 metres of the British entrenchments, but they were then forced to retreat from the murderous enemy gunfire. The burghers had to leave behind 50 dead men and 30 who were very badly wounded.

This was the end of the war in the western Transvaal and also the last important battle of the Anglo-Boer War.

CHAPTER X
PEACE

Dr A. Kuyper's missive

On 25 January 1902 Dr Abraham Kuyper, the Dutch Prime Minister, sent a diplomatic note to the British government offering his government's services as mediator between the British and the republican governments for an interchange of ideas on a peace agreement. Speaking through Lord Lansdowne, its Minister of Foreign Affairs, the British government politely refused the offer, saying that negotiations on the conclusion of peace should be conducted between the republican governments and Kitchener in his capacity as supreme commander of the British military forces.

The British then sent copies of the two missives to Kitchener. He in turn forwarded copies to the Transvaal government, but not to the government of the Free State.

The meeting at Klerksdorp

Acting President Schalk Burger sent a reply to Kitchener on 10 March, indicating that his government was prepared to engage in peace negotiations, but that it would first have to hold discussions with the Free State government. The Transvaal government had thus exchanged thoughts with Kitchener before consulting the Free State. Members of the Transvaal government were given the assurance of safe conduct to go to Kroonstad to try to get in touch with Steyn. He was eventually traced to De la Rey where he was receiving medical treatment.

A meeting was then held in Klerksdorp on 9 April. After Steyn had reiterated his stand that there could be no question of sacrificing the independence of the republics, it was decided to request a personal interview with Kitchener in Pretoria to establish what conditions the

British government was proposing for the peace settlement. In a letter to Kitchener the two governments indicated their readiness to conclude peace in terms of an agreement with Britain and to negotiate further on the matters of the franchise and equal status for the English and Dutch languages.

This meeting took place on 12 April. Milner was to attend some of the deliberations. On behalf of his government Kitchener refused pointblank to negotiate on the basis of the recognition of independence for the two republics. The members of the two governments replied that they could negotiate on sacrificing their independence only if they had authorisation from the people, that is the burghers in the field, to do so. It was then agreed that the burghers would choose a number of representatives who would meet at Vereeniging on 15 May. There they would decide whether, to enter into peace negotiations with the British government with or without recognition of republican independence.

The meeting at Vereeniging

On the appointed day 30 delegates each from the Free State and Transvaal commandos met outside Vereeniging to begin their deliberations. Smuts had also come from the Cape Colony to attend. The proceedings were to be conducted under the chairmanship of Beyers. One noteworthy absentee from the tent where the talks were held was Steyn, who was seriously ill with a muscular paralysis and had resigned as president. For three full days – from 15 to 17 May – the various delegates reported on the conditions in their parts of the country and expressed their opinions on whether the war should be continued. This was a highly controversial issue. Some delegates were clearly in favour of ending the struggle while others argued for its continuation. Two issues came under serious discussion, namely the situation of widespread devastation in both republics and the large number of women and children who had died in the concentration camps. It was eventually decided to authorise the two governments to negotiate with the representatives of the British government on the following conditions: the republican surrender of foreign ties, acceptance of a British protectorate, surrender of a portion of Transvaal territory – the delegates here had the Witwatersrand with its gold mines in mind – and the conclusion of a defensive alliance with Britain.

Delegates of the two republics submitted these proposals to Kitchener and Milner on 19 May. In the course of the discussions that followed the two British men made it very clear that they were not prepared to accept these conditions. It was obvious that as far as they were concerned negotiations could take place only on the basis of the complete surrender of republican independence. Nothing could change this.

Hertzog and Smuts were nominated to consult with Milner to draw up the terms whereby the two republics would abandon their independence and become part of the British empire. The three men completed their draft peace treaty by 21 May and the contents were sent by cablegram to the British government for approval.

These proceedings had taken a full week, so the representatives of the two governments were able to return to Vereeniging only on 28 May to submit the draft to the delegates.

On 29 May the discussions began again. The draft specified that the burghers of the two republics should lay down their arms and acknowledge King Edward VII of Britian as their sovereign. For its part, the British government undertook inter alia:

(a)   to allow school children to be educated in the Dutch language;

(b)   to grant self-government to the Transvaal and Free State as soon as circumstances allowed;

(c)   not to give the franchise to the black people; and

(d)   to pay an amount of £3 000 000 as compensation for the damage caused during the war to private property.

The discussions continued until 31 May. A number of delegates insisted that the draft should be rejected and the war resumed, but it was clear that the majority were in favour of peace. Ultimately it was approved by 54 votes to six that peace be signed in accordance with the conditions agreed upon in Pretoria.

The members of the two governments left for Pretoria and at five minutes past eleven the night of 31 May 1902 the peace treaty was signed, bringing the war to a close and signalling the end of independence for the two republics.

CHAPTER XI
THE WAR
AND THE OUTSIDE WORLD

Although the Anglo-Boer War played itself out within the boundaries of South Africa, it also had a measure of influence in the area of international relations. To understand the real significance of the war it is necessary to pay brief attention to its impact on conditions in the wider world. This influence was twofold in nature. Firstly, it can be seen in the military sphere and secondly in the area of international politics.

The military sphere

The way in which two tiny states offered a mighty international empire such dogged resistance for nearly three years made a substantial impression on other countries. As a result they began to study the strategy and military techniques used by the Boers. The rest of the world learnt from the Boers in three particular respects.

The first of these was the mobility of the commandos. Military observers were amazed to see how quickly the Boer commandos were able to move. The core of a European army had traditionally been its infantry or foot soldiers, so to the outside world the manner in which De Wet was able to cover hundreds of kilometres within a few days made a marked impression. Subsequently there were attempts to equal the mobility of a Boer commando, but this was only achieved after the introduction of mechanised weapons such as the tank.

The second aspect was the way in which the Boers made use of the natural terrain for the necessary cover so that they were out of the enemy's sight. The trenches that the republican forces had dug at Magersfontein and Colenso for instance, served as examples in the First World War when the Germans on the one hand, and the British and the French on the other, faced each other in trenches that stretched from the coast of Belgium to the border of Switzerland. The manner in which both sides attempted to keep their soldiers out of the enemy's view was a direct imitation of the methods of warfare used by the Boers in the Anglo-Boer War.

The third aspect was the remarkable fire power that even a tiny group of Boer sharpshooters could generate. A small number of burghers who were good shots were often able to halt a large British force and inflict heavy losses. This also had a role in the development of the machine gun which could be operated by two or three men and could fire hundreds of times per minute.

In yet another way the Anglo-Boer War had an impact on events that followed. The war in South Africa exposed large and serious shortcomings in the organisation and leadership of the British army. The fact that the forces of the British army, which had everything in their favour, needed almost three years to conquer two little republics was the cause of great concern in British military and political circles. It was with this in mind that Lord Haldane, who became Minister of War in 1905, made radical changes to the organisation of the British army.

Today it is generally admitted that the British army was able to carry out its operations successfully only because of the reforms Haldane had introduced. And most of these changes had their origin in the experience gained during the Anglo-Boer War.

International politics

When the Anglo-Boer War began in 1899, Britain still held the attitude that it should not enter into an alliance with any other European power. Lord Salisbury once referred to this as a policy of "splendid isolation". For a number of reasons in the years immediately preceding the outbreak of the war in South Africa, the relationship between Britain and the other most important European powers such as Germany, France and Russia was somewhat cool. When the war began, one of the major questions facing the British government was what these European powers would get up to while Britain had its hands tied in South Africa. The issue arose because these powers did nothing to conceal their glee over the trouble in which Britain found herself. There was little concern that the powers might interfere in the war in South Africa, because the British navy still controlled the seas and was indeed more than a match for the combined fleets of the other powers.

Among Afrikaners there was initially the belief that the European powers might intervene on their behalf, but this never came to fruition. By controlling the seas, Britain was able to isolate the war in South Africa from other world affairs. The other powers did indeed try once or twice to draw some advantage from the fact that Britain had to turn all its attention to the war in South Africa, but the relationships between them was so strained – Germany and France, for example, were arch rivals – that nothing much came of this.

It became obvious on two occasions that the European powers were not prepared to do anything on behalf of the Boer republics. The first opportunity was the arrival in Europe April 1900 of a three-man delegation comprising A. Fischer, C.H.Wessels and A.D.W. Wolmarans. They had been sent specifically to appeal to other powers to intervene in the war. But Kaiser Wilhelm II of Germany, for one, simply said that there was nothing he could do.

Nor did a visit to America produce anything positive. During a visit to Russia there was indeed a show of support in government circles, but it went no further than that.

The second occasion was Kruger's arrival in Europe in November 1900. The Dutch warship, the *Gelderland*, in which he had journeyed from Lourenço Marques (now Maputo) took him to the French harbour of Marseille on the Mediterranean Sea. He then travelled to Paris where the French certainly received him with great enthusiasm, but a request to the government that he be allowed to tell them about the plight of the two republics came to nothing. The French statesmen could not see their way clear to listen. Kruger wanted to go from Paris to Berlin, but when he arrived in Cologne he was told that Wilhelm II could not receive him. Kruger then departed for the Netherlands where he remained for the duration of the war.

Nevertheless the war in South Africa did have some influence on world affairs and two aspects can be mentioned here.

Firstly, the war made Britain realise that the era of "splendid isolation" was over. Britain needed allies. Germany had been its first choice as an ally, but the German government had laid down conditions that the British government could not meet. Then Britain started negotiations with France and in 1904 the well-known *Entente Cordiale* was concluded between them.

Secondly, a feeling of estrangement developed between Britain and Germany which became a contributing factor to the outbreak of the First World War in 1914. This estrangement between the two powers had already begun at the close of the nineteenth century. The fact that the German people made no secret of their sympathy for the two republics was a cause of great irritation in Britain and the two nations began to regard each other as enemies. Their political relationship was so negatively influenced that eventually even the statesmen on either side were exchanging harsh words. In 1902 at the end of the war in South Africa relations between Britain and Germany were decidedly less cordial than they had been in 1899 when the war had begun.

Despite the fact that none of these governments would do anything to help the republics, the people of Europe were strongly pro-Afrikaner. In countries such as the Netherlands, Germany, France and Russia there was widespread sympathy for the republican cause. In these countries various committees were established to spread propaganda in favour of the republics, to offer medical help to the burghers on commando and to provide assistance for the women and children in the concentration camps. In this way they provided a great service to the Afrikaner people.

CHAPTER XII
THE WAR AND SOUTH AFRICA

It goes without saying that the influence that the war had on South Africa was far greater than that experienced in other parts of the world.

With the signing of the Peace of Vereeniging on 31 May 1902 the whole of South Africa came under British rule. The most important implication of this was undoubtedly the fact that the political union of South Africa was made infinitely easier. The British statesmen and Milner, their representative in South Africa, now aspired to this union. When Chamberlain, the British Minister for the Colonies, visited South Africa in 1903, he placed great emphasis on this issue. South Africa had to become a political entity.

Milner took the first steps and by 1903 he had already placed the railways of the Transvaal and the Free State under joint management. An even more important move towards closer cooperation was his role in the formation of a customs union for the four colonies.

When Milner left South Africa in 1905 the desired union had not yet taken place. His work was to be continued by his successor, Lord Selborne. The most important step that Selborne took to promote the union of South Africa was the publication on 1 January 1907 of his well-known and very convincing memorandum that outlined the advantages of uniting the four colonies.

The aspirations for union were hampered by one particular issue. While the Cape Colony and Natal enjoyed self-governemt, this was not yet the case in the Transvaal and the Free State. They had initially been governed like crown colonies, with the residents having no voice at all in the administration. One of Britain's assurances to the two republics at Vereeniging in 1902 was that they would, as soon as possible, be given self-government. In both the Transvaal and the Free State the Afrikaners had begun their efforts to realise this as early as 1904. In the Transvaal men such as Botha, Smuts, Beyers and De la Rey met in Pretoria on

24 May 1904 to form a political organisation called Het Volk which aimed to secure a constitution for the Transvaal in which provision would be made for self-rule, in other words responsible government. On 2 December of the same year the Free Staters under the direction of men like Hertzog, De Wet and Fischer met in Brandfort and formed the Orangia Unie with the same objective.

Lord Milner

The British Conservative government was unsympathetic towards these aspirations for self-rule because they were afraid that the government in both the ex-republics would pass into the hands of the Afrikaners. In 1905 a constitution was drawn up for the Transvaal which made provision for representative government only, that is the Transvalers could choose their own legislative authority, but the executive authority would be completely independent of the legislature. This meant that the executive authority could not be brought down by the legislative authority. Most Transvalers were dissatisfied with this limited measure of self-rule and when the Conservative Party lost the British elections in December 1905 and had to make way for a Liberal government under Sir Henry Campbell-Bannerman, Smuts went to Britain to hold private talks with the most important members of the British cabinet. The result was that the constitution introduced by the Conservative government was rescinded and full self-government was granted to the Transvaal.

On 22 February 1907 the first general election was held and Het Volk gained a clear victory. Botha became prime minister. The Free State also received self-government a few months later. The election put the Orangia Unie in control and Fischer was named as premier. Now that all parts of South Africa had self-rule it was easier to negotiate about a political union. In 1908 decisive steps were taken which subsequently led to the realisation of this great ideal.

All four colonies chose a number of delegates who would gather in Durban on 2 October 1908 to negotiate on drafting a constitution for a united South Africa. This work was later continued in Cape Town and Bloemfontein. In terms of the constitution South Africa would become a union and not a federation. Both English and Dutch would be official languages: it was Hertzog and Steyn who were primarily responsible for the inclusion of this clause.

The draft constitution was then submitted to the British government which approved it without any amendments. The Union of South Africa thus came into being on 31 May 1910 — precisely eight years after the Peace of Vereeniging had been signed.

LIST OF ILLUSTRATIONS

LIST OF MAPS

INDEX